A Little Bit of Grace

A Spiritual Memoir

Divine Grace Buszka

Copyright © 2017 Divine Grace Buszka
All rights reserved.

A Little Bit of Grace is a work of creative non-fiction.
The events are portrayed to the best of the author's memory.
While all of the stories in this book are true, some names and
identifying details have been changed to protect the privacy
of the people involved.

For Keoni.
Thank you for meeting me here.
For waking me up and being my hero.
I love you infinity.

Acknowledgments

To Steve, thank you for always believing in me and for *seeing* me. To Donna and Mark, thank you for never allowing me to give up and for always inspiring me to rise. I love you all.

To Tracy, thank you for your mentorship, commitment to helping me hone my messages and getting me to *the finish line*.

To the Ascended Masters, the I Am Presence and the Angels who have always guided me and given me assistance, thank you. My journey to enlightenment has been and continues to be a magical one. With the presence of these Ascended Beings in my life, I humbly bow in reverence, gratitude and honor. Thank you for allowing me to share these stories and messages.

I wasn't quite ready for more challenges, but life's flow is non-stop. One can't refuse to move and still expect to be perfectly in-sync with it.
DGB

Contents

Chapter 1 1
Chapter 2 5
Chapter 3 15
Chapter 4 21
Chapter 5 29
Chapter 6 37
Chapter 7 43
Chapter 8 51
Chapter 9 57
Chapter 10 65
Chapter 11 73
Chapter 12 81
Chapter 13 89
Chapter 14 97
Chapter 15 109
Chapter 16 121
Chapter 17 129
Chapter 18 135
Chapter 19 147
Chapter 20 153
Chapter 21 163
Chapter 22 171
Chapter 23 181
Chapter 24 197
Chapter 25 211
Epilogue 217

Chapter 1

"I'm sorry, ma'am, but you're not going to be able to get on the ship."

Words I wasn't expecting to hear that afternoon. I was getting married in three days in Mexico. My luggage was on board along with half of my wedding guests, and the other half were staring blankly at me. I *needed* to get on the ship—the cruise ship that was supposed to take me to *my* wedding—but as I stood there, wedding dress in one hand, purse and cruise ticket in the other, this lady said I couldn't.

Well... shit, I felt like I had just crashed into a brick wall. God, Universe, Source, anyone up there who's listening, anyone period, what do I do now?!

I had no valid passport; it had been lost during the move to our new home. I couldn't request a new passport either, because... well... my citizenship papers had also been lost, along with other documents that confirmed my identity. It was a mess I had tried figuring out some months prior, with trips to the immigration office to get a copy of my certificate of citizenship to prove I had become an American. That was the only way I could replace my passport and ultimately, travel out of the country. I was told that the process to prepare and collect all the paperwork would take a lot more time than I had before my trip.

However, it had appeared resolved a month earlier, when the cruise line said they would allow me to get on the ship as long as I had a U.S. government identification card (like my driver's license) and that the U.S. Customs and Border Protection (CBP) agents would take care of the rest. They assured me that I would be able to get on the ship and sail down to Mexico and back. Well, of course, with my luck, or lack of it that day, as I handed the cruise ticket agent what they had asked for, they responded that they couldn't confirm my citizenship with CBP because it was Sunday, and the offices had closed early that day.

I think it was about this time when it felt like the world stopped briefly. The Universe called "time out," and I benched myself momentarily from this game of life to figure my way out of this, no matter how impossible it seemed.

Paul and I had decided to have a destination wedding in Cabo San Lucas, Mexico. Inviting only about forty of our family and closest friends, it was going to be an intimate wedding, heartfelt and beautiful. With a ceremony on the shore looking out to the turquoise-blue ocean, our son was to be our little ring bearer. I looked forward to that moment when I would finally walk down the aisle to him and celebrate our union as husband and wife. After six years of all sorts of crazy-beautiful, a baby, and a young kind of love, I would finally be *his* wife.

Looking back, I almost feel like we were checking off an item from a "how to do life correctly" list. There was a lot of pressure and not a lot of clarity—a bad combo for making one of the biggest decisions of your life. Being told that I couldn't board the ship might have been the Universe telling me: you don't have to do this. Creating an unexpected detour may have been a glaring sign (that I didn't heed), to pay attention to the months, or even years, of unsettled emotions and doubt regarding my and Paul's relationship.

I stood there in my internal time out, pretending I had paused life, but in reality, time was ticking, and my guests (still staring at me for answers) would shortly need to board the ship which would soon set sail. My groom-to-be and my dad continued to ask cruise staff personnel for ways around this or if they could just allow me on the ship anyway, which they obviously weren't going to do. I couldn't sail with them, I couldn't fly there without a passport, and I couldn't drive there to arrive on time. There were seemingly infinite roadblocks on all levels that kept me from continuing ahead. I *really* should have taken this as a sign.

But as stubborn as I was, I told the Universe: "No."

I decided to take charge. Ultimately I was in control; however, I did ask Spirit for help and trusted that I would be given further guidance.

The Universe took me aside (so it seemed), and asked, "Are you sure, and we mean, are you *really* sure you want to go through with *this*?"

And in that split second of deciding: "Yes, I'm pretty damn right sure I want to go through with this—perhaps go on an unplanned adventure that will hopefully take me to my desired destination," I got my answer.

Loud and clear, I heard the Universe tell me, "Tell your groom-to-be and your family and friends to board the ship. Tell them to have fun at sea and promise them that you'll meet them there in a couple days' time. Promise them that there will be a wedding. Say good-bye to them and then, call Carlos. We promise you'll get on the ship. You'll go through a lot to get there, but you'll make it. You'll get on the ship in the end. But first, call Carlos…"

In my momentary blankness, I had received an answer from somewhere beyond the veils. I trusted, without a doubt, my gut feeling, my intuition, and the words given to me from guides on the other side. I had to go with it, no matter how random, crazy, or wrong it may have appeared. I asked for guidance; they had responded. So I trusted. Faith is blind. And at times like this, you need to hold on and continue believing. I surrendered to the flow, which is scary as hell sometimes, and this was definitely one of those times.

The words that finally came out of my mouth would make me seem as if I had gone mad. But if they only knew how certain I was that *this* was the way... they, too, would not have had reservations about the plan.

"Please, everyone, get on the ship. Enjoy the next couple of days at sea, and I'll meet you guys in Cabo. I promise."

They definitely did not expect to hear *those* words from the bride, who at the moment had no possible way of getting there. They looked at me with a sort of awe—maybe because I was so calm. But I think it was more so that what I had blurted out seemed completely ridiculous.

"You really want us to get on the ship, and you promise you'll meet us there?" they chorused.

They probably believed there wouldn't be a wedding, and because they had paid for a cruise, figured they might as well get on the ship and enjoy a good vacation.

I requested that my groom-to-be (who asked numerous times to stay with me), get on the ship in order to keep our guests company and to watch over our child as I journeyed over a different way. In fact, there were a couple people who asked to remain with me, but I only wanted one of my maids of honor. Who else to have a crazy adventure with than an awesome pal?! I mean, I definitely knew it was going to be a *crazy* adventure, trying to get somewhere with a staggering mountain of obstacles and time, good ol' sweet time, racing against me.

As Kayla and I left the cruise terminal, I felt confident. I would get there, no matter what it took!

And then, I heard the horns of the ship and saw it slowly inch away from the harbor, and my heart dropped a million miles below existence. *What the hell was I thinking?! I'm supposed to be on that ship!*

Chapter 2

Tear after tear rolled down my cheeks. I felt like an utter failure. I was supposed to be on that ship, and there I was – NOT on that ship – and crying over losing a game of tug of war with fate.

And then I heard it again, loud and clear, "Call Carlos," (and maybe even "Okay, Grace, stop being a wuss"). Like a shot of adrenaline waking me up, I took a deep breath and diverted my attention to my oversized purse, scrambling to find my phone. *Thank you for the reminder, Universe. But really? Carlos?* I hadn't spoken to him in about a year, not since he had congratulated me on my engagement. I had worked with him at a bank a handful of years ago and we'd remained friends. Despite our continued connection, it was still beyond random, because we rarely communicated or touched base with one another, but at that point I was going to take whatever option or guidance there was. I hurriedly dialed his number.

Right away he picked up. After I finished telling him what happened, a fresh round of crying erupted.

All I heard from the other end was laughter.

As I struggled to keep from cursing him out, he quickly took a couple steps back and confirmed the story to make sure he had heard accurately. "So wait, dude, you're trying to get to Cabo, and out of all the people on your contact list, you called me?! That's really funny because my family and I are flying out to Cabo *tomorrow*—"

"Wait, what?!" I was in shock, but kinda not. Of course I'd heard right when Spirit had instructed me to call him. I mean, this thing called intuition, magic, guides beyond this physical world, *maybe* it's all true!

Dammit, Grace, of course it is.

This was yet another instance when the Universe had interjected and proven its mighty and kind existence. And again, I was still somewhat questioning. How many signs, how many validations, do we really need?! But, of course, we're human down here. Our fears, doubts, and insecurities get in the way; we forget truth. If we only knew how powerful we really are...

Carlos continued on, somewhat disbelieving (I could hear it in his voice).

"Okay, I'll tell you what, let me call you back. Give me five minutes to ask around and see what we can do to get you there."

I had no doubt he'd call me back, that he *was* asking the plethora of individuals in his network to see what we could do. And yes, this whole thing seemed impossible, because what kind of people in their right mind decide to take this route? Probably not a lot – maybe just me. But because the Universe had whispered into my ear to call Carlos and because he was coincidentally flying to Cabo the next day, there was no room for questioning. This huge synchronicity was confirmation that I had an invisible army on the other side guiding me, and it was impossible to fail. I needed to focus on my *why* and not on *how* I was going to get there. The details that made up the how, the logistics, they were going to magically come together if I focused on my intention and purpose, *my why*. This I believed strongly.

As promised, five minutes later, Carlos called back. I listened intently.

"Okay, after speaking with a few of my friends, here's what we've got. We have three options here. Option one, go home, and purchase a ticket for the flight that my family and I are taking. It flies out of Tijuana. There are still available seats, so hurry! Print your tickets out. Next, make an appointment for the earliest time slot tomorrow morning with the passport agency in downtown San Diego. Bring whatever legal paperwork you have that might help you get a passport. Bring the printed plane tickets with you to the passport agency. If you tell them that you have flights and plans to leave the country and show them proof, they'll be more apt to help you get a passport. Next, call the shuttle company and arrange your ride to the Tijuana airport for our 3pm takeoff. Then, go to Kinkos and get pictures taken for the passport—that they'll *hopefully* give you tomorrow morning. Lastly, eat a good dinner and get some sleep. You've got a lot of work ahead of you tomorrow.

"That's option one. Option two, if they don't give you a passport, get on the shuttle anyway, get to Tijuana, and get on the plane. We'll get to Cabo a day before the ship arrives. You'll have time to get to the U.S. embassy. Tell them that you are a U.S. citizen and that you've lost your passport while traveling. They'll be able to confirm your citizenship right away and give you a passport. You'll be able to walk down the aisle, say "I do," and cruise back up with your wedding party, no problem.

"And if that doesn't work, we'll go with option three. Option three, if they don't give you a passport at the U.S. embassy in Cabo, walk down the aisle anyway, say "I do," and then kiss your new husband goodbye as he and your wedding party board the ship to cruise back home while you fly back to Tijuana. At the border, as you re-enter the United States, although you won't have a passport (and you'll spend a handful of hours most likely getting interrogated), they will probably and eventually be able to confirm your citizenship, and you'll be able to re-enter the United States.

"So what do you say…? Let's do this."

As he finally finished, he reassured me that it would all work out and even mentioned examples of people he knew that had used those strategies successfully.

Okay, I'm not going to fail!

It was about 5pm, and the clock was ticking. Kayla and I hurried on home, and I quickly got online to purchase plane tickets through Volaris Airlines. As I was purchasing the tickets, I remember pausing at the part where it asked if these were going to be one-way tickets. I looked up at Kayla and thought, *Yes, of course. We're getting on that ship and cruising back up with them, because, well, everything will work out. I'll get a passport tomorrow, and all will be good.* I'm not sure if my positivity at the time was because I trusted that it would work out, or if I was trying to persuade myself that it would. Either way, it helped keep the energy light and helped me stay confident, which is sometimes all that one needs in the pursuit of combating fear.

After purchasing our tickets and printing them out, we quickly made an appointment with the passport agency and reserved a shuttle for pick up at my home and delivery to the Tijuana airport across the border the next day. Soon after, we rushed to Kinkos for passport pictures. It was one checklist item after the other. I could hear the clock ticking in my head as I hurried along. There was no room for dilly-dallying or allowing myself to wallow in my sadness from a couple hours before, or even entertain doubts and fears of not being able to attend my own wedding. I had to focus and continue on with determination and unyielding confidence that I was going to get on that ship.

After accomplishing the tasks on our list to secure a successful day ahead, it was time to feast. Similar to a last meal preceding a fierce battle (before I went face-to-face with fear's greatest minions), I wanted this meal to be appropriate to herald soon-to-come glory. So, of course, I chose pizza, because, well, pizza is always a good idea. We drove to my favorite pizza parlor. Although I was getting married in a few days and needed to fit into my wedding dress, at this point I didn't care about anything else but eating a really good pie.

As if it were a pre-victory supper, I scarfed down my fave slices and more bread on top of that, something a bride-to-be doesn't usually partake in a few days before being zipped up in her white dress.

Before calling it a night, I phoned my groom. Briefly, I told him the plan. I could tell he was saddened by the situation as a whole, and in his energy, I felt his doubts. I reassured him that it would work out. He also did his best to reassure me that he *did* believe in me.

"Well, you always make things happen," he reminded me (and probably himself).

He constantly told me this. And if anything, I needed to hear it that night; because although deep down I knew there wasn't anything in my life I couldn't make happen, doubt scurried up and down my spine trying to persuade me otherwise. But! I refused the outcome that was opposite of my happiness, and onward I went.

Waking up early to get downtown in time for our appointment, I felt alert and energized despite the lack of sleep from the night before. I wasn't sure if it was excitement or anxiety that jolted through me, waking me up to the stark reality of "go time." I might win, and I might lose. But I wasn't going to walk away without a fight. One which might be brutal. But for what I was fighting for, it was worth it.

We made it on time in spite of Monday morning traffic. Walking up to the window, all I could think was: *Please, God, be here with me. Fill me with your grace.* As I started to explain my situation and showed them my tickets, it became obvious — they weren't going to help me!

"You have no evidence that proves your citizenship – or even your identity," the clerk said, deadpan.

Here it was. Coming at me like a full-speed train on steroids; I had lost.

I didn't have enough documentation to go forth. *I* wasn't enough. Oh no, there's that limiting belief: I am not enough.

Waaawaaawaaa... wait, was I really going to allow myself to quit right then and there? No, I had more to do. I knew it. That was a small blow; it barely grazed my being. I realized that I was still standing.

I pulled out the letter I had gotten from the immigration office confirming that I had done my due diligence and pursued that avenue as well. The letter stated that they were in the process of collecting the paperwork that confirmed my citizenship. I watched the passport agency employee reading it – scrutinizing his face for information. This guy could have been a wiz at poker. The room felt crowded, brimming with antsy and bored individuals who waited to be called up to a window. I felt like I was at a mini DMV. I couldn't wait to get out of there and be done with all of this.

"Okay," he said.

Huh? Could it have been that simple? Why am I questioning? Take it, Grace, just take it! So I did.

"Your passport will be ready in two hours."

Perfect, we'll have enough time to make it home for the shuttle pickup.

Round one, in the clear! *Everything* was in the clear. I could leisurely continue my morning as I waited for my passport to get processed. I was on cloud nine. *Is that Heaven's symphony playing in the background celebrating my success? Yes it is.*

Kayla and I walked down a few blocks to grab some well-deserved breakfast at a nearby French bakery. While waiting for the server to take our orders, I called the cruise line to let them know that I hadn't boarded the ship in San Diego, but I'd be able to, the next morning in Cabo.

Our French toast was on its way (I know, more carbs), and before it arrived my phone rang. *Well, that was fast – passport done already?*

"Hello. You were just in our office. Can you please give me the confirmation number you received from the immigration offices for the order they put in to get your paperwork?"

"Um...unfortunately, I didn't receive a confirmation number."

"Oh. How much did you pay for the order?"

"Uh, I wasn't asked to pay for the order."

"Well, without the confirmation number, we can't proceed with processing your passport."

"Really? Hold on a minute, please."

I motioned to Kayla that I needed to get back to the passport agency, and I would meet her there. Still on the phone with the guy, I quickly got a cab and zipped back to the office.

We went over how I hadn't been charged for the order and hadn't received any kind of confirmation number either. We brainstormed other options for working around this issue.

"The only way to go forward will be to call the immigration office and pay for the order over the phone. Then we'll use that confirmation number to finish processing your passport," the staff-person said.

Well this blindsided me. Like a surprise jab from an opponent I wasn't expecting, from behind.

Sitting in the lobby, I quickly got a hold of Immigration. After explaining my crazy situation to the rep on the other line, this was the news: Unfortunately, you can't make a payment over the phone or even online.

Brick wall and dead end once again.

Tic tic toc. The option to walk over to the immigration office a handful of blocks away, wait in line, get some sort of assistance, and return to the passport agency in time to get my passport processed and printed was nearly impossible. Time was a huge opponent. I couldn't physically stop time. That would be complete and utter magic, and I wasn't at that level yet.

Or was I?

I sat on a bench in the lobby of the passport agency thinking about how close I had come. As I slowly accepted failure,

I heard, "Really?! You've come this far. You're going to quit now? You're here already, might as well get back on the tenth floor to speak up for yourself." Although I felt puny, the message of the voice within empowered me to get up anyway and march my little butt back upstairs. I'm not sure if I shook out of nervousness or if it was really that cold in the building, but my whole body sort of trembled. I could feel that pit in my stomach fill with fear. I couldn't entertain that emotion. I needed to refocus on my purpose. I was going to at least speak my *truth,* whatever it was at that point.

Still shaking with nervousness and not really knowing what to say, I walked up to the window. Immediately, he asked how much it had cost for the order. I told him what it was; I knew the amount due to my earlier conversation with the immigration office. And then he asked me what my confirmation number was. And before I could utter a particle of speech, I prayed: *Spirit, be present and be my voice.*

Without the answer he was looking for, all I had left was my truth, and I needed to speak it. "I don't know. I don't know what the confirmation number is because I wasn't able to pay for it over the phone. However, what I do know is that I'm going to Cabo for love—to marry the man I adore and whom I have loved and fought to be with for years. And although you don't know who I am and I don't know who you are, what I do know is that what we are truly made of is that which is Love in its entirety. *That's* what I know, and that's what my whole being believes in. And of all the things that you believe in on a daily basis, today, just for today, I'm asking you to believe in Love—to believe and to trust in that which you are. That's all."

God, did I really just say that? He's probably thinking, "What a bunch of..."

He eyed me with a sincere look and quietly handed me a blank piece of paper.

"Write down why you need to travel to Cabo and any

other details pertaining to your trip."

I felt like someone had called overtime, and there I was, given another chance to win this.

I quickly wrote out the details of my trip and handed it to him.

"I need to get approval from my manager. Be right back."

He left his counter, and I closed my eyes, put my hands in prayer position, and prayed to God and the other Ascended Hosts of Light available at that point in time: *Hear my plea for help.* I could feel my heart almost beat out of my chest. And all I could think was *Love, Love, Love,* **Love***. Please, Love, be present with me.*

While in the middle of my love mantra, I heard tapping on the window.

"Divine Grace. Ms. Divine Grace." He was back. "Good news, we'll go ahead and process your passport!"

YES!!!! I swear my heart leaped out of my chest in jubilation.

"Come back in a couple of hours, and you'll be all set," he said, smiling."

Wait...what? I heard the Universe pause the music again—no – it was more like it screeched to a halt.

I can't come back in a couple of hours; I need to be home to be picked up by the shuttle in less than a couple of hours.

"Is there any way around this time table?!" I asked, explaining.

"Don't worry; I think it'll be okay. I can't guarantee it, but there's a very good chance it'll be done in forty-five minutes. I'll push it through as extra urgent."

And optimism was enough to help shift the energies of an unpleasant situation.

Kayla and I paced the halls of the office building. Forty-five minutes isn't usually a long time, but this might have been the longest forty-five minutes of my life. At exactly the end of forty-five minutes, I marched back up to the window. The guy sifted through files and folders, and I could tell he was about to tell me that it wasn't ready, when someone from behind him dropped off an envelope marked "urgent" in red letters. He did a double-take, and thank God he did, because in that envelope was indeed *my passport*.

I had done it! I had overcome the impossible and was about to cheat time. I was beyond grateful, knowing that I had definitely been divinely guided to get to that point. Kayla and I whooped with joy as we hurried back to our car and back home. She was the cheerleader I needed. Someone to stay positive and create more sweet energy of hope and optimism. God bless Kayla's heart for having decided to go on this wild adventure with me. I would not have been as optimistic and determined if she had not been present.

On our way back home, I remember speeding down Highway 15 trying to get ahead of time. A particular song was playing: Florence and the Machine's "Dog Days Are Over." I blasted it as loud as I could. Dog days *were* over. Someone had finally brought me the horses, and I was on my way down to Mexico, horses and all. I had beat the system, and it was so damn good to feel free. Liberated from fear, the amount of triumphant glory that ran through my veins made me feel untouchable. I was in the presence of Gods guiding me ever so safely to my destination. I trusted this.

Chapter 3

When we arrived home, the shuttle was waiting in the driveway. I only had time to run upstairs to grab my wedding dress. Yep, a close call, but it was like the winning basket shot or the Hail Mary out of nowhere at the last second. It still counted, *and* it won the game.

I had received messages from friends and family urging me not to try to get to Cabo because crossing the border into Tijuana at that time was thought to be dangerous. They suggested I wait for my party to get home and have the wedding there instead. Also, without proper identification, they were afraid that I would get stuck somewhere and not make it to Cabo or back across the border. Their fears were valid. But I knew better than to give in to those fears and doubts. On our way across the border to the Tijuana airport, I beamed; I was feeling so happy and excited.

I had not communicated with anyone on the ship since the night before, so at this point, they had no idea what was happening. I'm pretty sure their assumption by then was that there wasn't going to be a wedding and the best thing to do was continue enjoying their vacation. I didn't blame them. I probably would have thought the same. But, fortunately, it wasn't going to turn out that way. I was going to make it happen. There *would* be a wedding.

As I rushed into the airport, I spotted Carlos and his family. I wish I'd had my camera to capture the look on his face. At first, almost as if he had seen a ghost, he wore a bewildered expression, completely surprised. And then that look transformed to an expression of joy, all smiles and laughter—the kind when you're so happy that a smile just doesn't do it, so then your body creates laughter too.

"Dude!!! You made it!!! Wow, you really made it! I can't believe it! But that's awesome, dude! You actually made it with a passport and all. That's awesome! Let's get to Cabo!"

It turned out that Carlos had only hyped up the options to make me believe that it would work out. Although he had felt a little doubtful himself, the faith he had shown had in turn reassured me, which had set the mindset of success, given me faith, and allowed me to trust that I would succeed. This helped me shift the energy in the beginning, thus creating ultimate victory.

There had been no other way for me but to turn inward and hold on to faith. That *was* the way, and because I believed in it with complete and utter knowing, it worked and fulfilled the intention I had set forth.

Match the vibration of that which you want to manifest. Shift the energy and heighten the frequencies by shifting your mindset and taking on a new perspective. No matter what, I would make my wedding happen. I matched the energy of Love and there it was, happening before my eyes…

As the plane took off, I rested easy. *Thank you, Spirit, thank you, thank you, thank you.* I felt divinely guided and all was well.

Finally getting to Cabo, we parted ways with Carlos and his family while thanking him a million times over. As we walked out of the airport, we decided to buy a couple cervezas at the beverage stand planted outside the airport. It was the best damn Pacifico I had ever tasted. Cold, refreshing, and quite the reward after a long day of battling the rulers of fate, which I realized by then was actually my own God Self.

After sipping away on our frosty beers, Kayla and I walked off—not really knowing where we were walking off to—and realized that in the midst of the passport fiasco, we had forgotten to make sure we had a place to stay for the night. Since we had flown in a day before the cruise ship would dock, our accommodations at the resort weren't until the next evening. I knew the wedding resort was completely booked, and any suddenly available rooms would have cost much more than my budget would have tolerated. There was also a political event going on in Cabo that particular week; therefore *most* hotels were fully booked. However, I remembered our wedding coordinator mentioning, a couple weeks ago, that the sister hotel next door might have availability (when I had asked her about rooms for a few wedding guests flying in). Chances were slim, but it was worth a try.

As we got to the hotel, I remember praying: *Spirit, please, please, be here with me. Let them have available rooms we could stay in for the night. God in me, see that this is fulfilled.*

I walked up to the front desk, and just as I'd feared, the concierge told us that no rooms were available, apart from those excessively priced.

"All we need is a room for tonight," I said. I found myself speaking my truth again, from my heart to hers, sharing my story as to how I had gotten there and why. I lifted up my hand to show her my wedding dress.

"Apart from this, all I have is my purse." I gave her the kind of smile that said, "Look, lady, this is all I got, and I'm praying for rain here in what seems like a drought because I've got nothing, nothing else."

She smiled back, verifying that she understood me and motioned me to wait a bit. As she walked away to talk to her manager, I continued to pray. *Please, please, Love. Love, be here now.*

She returned, all smiles – a positive sign there would be something good for us. Lo and behold, there was one available room for the evening that she could give us for a small fee, but it only had partial ocean views and a queen bed.

"Wow, that's more than perfect! We'll take it!" I said immediately.

When you're given an opportunity or gift from the Universe, you say yes to it right away. As soon as you hesitate and think about it, it's no longer yours. This room was offered, so I dared not close the doors of chance.

Given the price of the room, I assumed it would be basic in quality but figured it would do for the evening. Unlocking the door, we took a couple steps inside.

Oh my God! It was a spectacular suite with two queen beds, a lounge, and balcony that had full-on ocean views. No wonder she'd been smiling and chuckling. She had just hooked it up! I was in deep gratitude and excitement that night knowing that tomorrow I'd be able to finally get on the ship.

The next morning, we found our way to the dock and enjoyed a simple breakfast by the water as we waited for the cruise ship to allow people on and off. The sun was high in the sky and shone perfectly, revealing the hustling life of the popular vacation spot. We watched the locals prepare themselves to welcome and entertain the crowds that would soon fill every pocket of the harbor. When it was finally time, we walked over.

"Hi. I called the cruise line yesterday to let them know I'd be getting on the ship, here in Cabo," I said.

They verified the information and gave me a thumbs up.

"But we cannot permit your friend to go aboard. According to the paperwork, it says that she got on in San Diego."

"I checked in at the San Diego port," Kayla said. "But then when Divine had this problem, I said I'd stay with her."

"I'm sorry, but there's no indication that you didn't board the ship."

"We just forgot to tell them," I said. "But she can show you her passport, and you'll see that it's her."

"Rules. You can go aboard, verify the situation with the staff, and they have to give us the green light to let her on."

So there I was at the very end, and although I'd had a

companion the whole time—someone to comfort me when I'd allowed fear in my head and my heart, someone who'd cheered me on and strengthened my faith throughout the journey, who'd never left my side—I was being made to complete the journey on my own. I looked up at Spirit and nodded, thinking, *Of course. You're making me go about this last stretch alone. I don't know whether to thank you or shake my head at you right now, Universe.* It felt like one of those love taps; although annoying, it was filled with Love and a potentially great realization regarding my journey and myself. It would no doubt empower me with the sweet reminder that, our paths may be filled with people who accompany us, but in the end, it's up to us to walk across that finish line - alone. As I sat in the small boat enroute to the ship, I couldn't help but tear up, overwhelmed with emotions of Love and elation in concluding my journey. I was almost in denial of the fact that I'd made this happen. I felt like I'd performed *magic*. My body was physically reacting to this by crying happy tears, which isn't something it does very often. I'm pretty sure the driver of the boat and the guy next to him felt awkward, but thank you, guys, for being present and allowing me to indulge in that moment of pure joy.

    Mind you, no one on the ship nor back home had any idea that I had arrived, and to top it off, my cell phone had no service, so I couldn't get in contact with anyone on the ship or back home. Regardless, I needed to find my groom, our son, and the rest of our wedding party among the thousands of individuals on board. First, I walked over to the front desk to take care of the Kayla situation. Next, I asked them to call the rooms of my wedding party. None of them answered. The only thing to do was explore the ship and hopefully find someone, anyone familiar.

    Ironically, as I stepped away from the front desk, about to start my search, I spotted my cousin, Missy, and our friend, Tina, walking through the lobby. Their surprised expressions were amusing to see. After a quick summary of how I'd gotten on the ship, they told me to head to the cafeteria on the ninth level, where everyone was having breakfast.

Missy and Tina walked towards the set of elevators on the side. For some reason, though, a particular elevator on the opposite wall was calling to me. After listening to my intuition this whole time and having been led correctly, I knew to follow this strong pull once more. We walked over to the other set of elevators and took one of those instead.

Reaching the ninth level of this gigantic floating city, I calmly exited the elevator. Intuitively, I felt I should take a couple steps to the right, and hurrah! Across from me, from the very point where I stood, was my groom and the rest of my party eating breakfast.

Paul stood up, looking utterly disappointed. (His father had just told him that he didn't think the wedding was going to go through.) And as he rose from his seat, he looked up, and our eyes connected. Disappointment dissipated, replaced by a look of complete surprise and awe. As it sank in that it was really me, I could feel the energy of joy take over his being. When everyone else also realized that it was me, physically on the ship, they couldn't believe it. My whole party was in complete shock that I had been able to make it happen. After hugs and tears of joy overfilled our space, we rightfully announced that, yes, indeed, there *would* be a wedding!

The following day we were joined together in matrimony. Just as I had imagined: the beautiful turquoise-blue ocean in the background, the sun beaming with warmth and luster in a cloudless azure sky, and the sandy aisle that I finally walked down to say, "I do." It was all that I had imagined, but more perfect because it was real and no longer a vision I had held in my mind for so long. Our son got to be our ring bearer. We sealed it with a kiss and celebrated our great feat throughout the day and on the ship cruising back home. Spirit was right, I would go through a lot and have many challenges, but in the end—I got on the ship!

Chapter 4

After the wedding, I thought life was complete.

Well, the cold and abrupt realization was that it was completely *incomplete*. I thought I was entering the phase when life would be sweetly lived out behind a white picket fence. I would be happily married, happily having more kids, happily living in a home my husband chose, and happily living out my passion. I felt like I had accomplished everything that would afford me a life beyond my wildest dreams. From a distance, it looked perfect. I had finally played by the rules, and maybe someone somewhere, at long last, thought I was good enough to be deemed worthy of approval and happiness. I felt like it was *supposed* to feel good—the marriage, the home, the contentment, every bit of it. This was supposed to fill up the deepest voids within me. But what I *didn't* feel was: whole, complete, honest, and happy. I had settled for a vanilla life, not the mocha-swirl, cherry-on-top one I had ambitiously been seeking.

Actually, there was no flavor, because I realized I was no longer in love with the person I shared my life with. Maybe the years of fighting, hurt, and utter loneliness took their toll; the multitude of times I was conditioned to think horribly of myself, that I was not good enough to be his wife or even the mother of his child; the many instances when I felt unappreciated or worthless. Or maybe, just maybe, it was simply because we had evolved out of the relationship, period. I had not fallen in love with or fancied another and neither had he. For whatever reason, the relationship no longer resonated with our guiding, inner compasses.

Did I still love him? Of course I did. I loved him more than ever, just as I loved myself in a new, deeper way. And because of that love for him and this newfound Self-love I was practicing, I wanted to give us freedom – the chance to find the kind of love that would truly fulfill our beings. It was clear we were incapable of doing so for one another. I knew, however, this generosity would not be taken well by him nor anyone else who lacked an understanding of the whole picture.

Here I was, sulking in my misery, avoiding the truth… and myself. Couldn't go around this – had to go through it. A little over a year and a half after I journeyed to Cabo to finally say "I do" to my groom, I woke up in a disastrous and complicated situation. This precipitated the move out of my husband's home and in with my dad and two younger siblings.

A mess internally, I attempted to keep my surface image well put together, or at least I thought it looked that way. I told people that I was happy with this decision. I *was* happy with it, but its consequences totally took me out of my comfort zone and back down to rock bottom, which I *wasn't* extremely happy about. Although deeply grateful for being able to stay at my dad's, sharing a room with my younger sister and sleeping on an air mattress on the floor gave me more humility than I had expected, but it was probably what I needed at the time. I had brought myself to that point in my life. There was no one else to blame nor an excuse to allow me to skip out on holding accountability. For some reason, as uncomfortable and miserable as I felt, I knew that was the way to go at the moment. No backing out. I needed to make things right, not just for me, but for *him*, my son. I wanted to show him the rewards that sacrifice, bravery, and following your heart brought. However, at that time, reality only delivered sadness, fear, doubts, and a brokenness deep within my being that I was incapable of relieving. I also wanted to show my son what true love between two people looked like. But in that state, the only thing I showed him was relentless pain—

relentless in letting me be, that is.

Being at the lowest edge of my life was not a foreign place. I had started there well before I even knew there was anything above it. I was pretty much used to that feeling of despair, feeling empty and broken, where you are existing solely in survival mode, except I didn't want to travel back there...

I entered the world in the middle of a raging storm. (Could my birth into this particular lifetime be any more melodramatic?) Rain and wind whipped against coconut trees and the land in a rural, provincial town in the Philippines.

Since it had become too late to take my mother to the hospital, I was born the old-fashioned way – with a midwife, my grandmothers, a bowl of warm water, and a handful of towels. There were no drugs to numb the pain or the emotions. My strong mother was completely awake and aware, immersed in what this sacred experience had to offer. While the elements battled in the atmosphere and the heavens occasionally roared with pride, my mother tirelessly pushed me out of her womb and into the world.

My poor father anxiously waited outside of the room, not knowing what would come of this or what being a parent would call forth from him. The test was immediate. I had been born slightly crippled with my right foot turned inwards. My father created a brace out of cardboard and cloth for my tiny foot to straighten out so I could walk when it was time. He put a warm compress on it every night and massaged it until my foot was properly in place and I was deemed normal.

I'm pretty sure he gently broke it in order to set it straight, and I've had a weak right ankle ever since. Ironically, as a little kid, I never sat still. I was always walking, running, or climbing on something. And now, I'm a runner and still pretty active on my feet. So much for a weakness that would have stunted me. Pretty much demolished that obstacle right away. Thanks, Dad. Little did I know that he'd set the stage for me: whatever challenge stood in my way, I would triumph, no matter how impossible it seemed. One point for Grace. Universe, I'll see you next round.

Returning to my humble upbringing...my story started quietly with the innocence and purity inherent in a sweet, simple life, maybe to show me that love *does* exist (before it faded from my memory). It was me, my mom, and my dad - complete, together, and happy. I spent the first four and a half years of my life running around barefoot and climbing as many trees as I could. I'd scurry to the top of a guava tree, wearing nothing but flip flops, and survey the tree for fruit. Not wanting to give into fear as I sat on the highest branch, I didn't dare look down, but took in the view around me while eating guavas plucked on the climb up. I looked out across rooftops and the plaza across the street where children played all day long. Although I sat high up (possibly dangerous for a small lad like me to sit there longer than I'd promised my mom), I felt safe. Invincible, actually, and free. Before climbing down, pockets filled with guavas, I'd take it all in before my feet hit the ground again and I no longer felt like a god. Life was uncomplicated. The beauty of the day lingered into the evening, never in a rush to become tomorrow. Energy flowed differently. It was as if life was lived in the present: no hurting over the past or worrying about the future. There was a strong appreciation for breath—simply having breath.

Which was a fortunate attitude, as we didn't have much and neither did the rest of the town, but we had each other, and that was enough. We didn't wear fancy outfits (and when I say fancy, I mean anything that didn't have holes), except during special occasions like birthdays, Christmas, and the annual fiesta, which was a huge deal to the town.

Life wasn't luxurious, but deep connection with family and community, appreciation of life, the joy of being free from stresses and pressures I would soon discover moving to America- was all I needed to grow up. This life felt more real than I ever felt in my adolescent years living in the States.

So here are some of my favorite memories from my

unique, idyllic early childhood: Dad and I playing hide and go seek; me sitting on my rocking chair singing as he played the guitar while Mom cleaned up after dinner; taking afternoon naps with Mom, followed by a walk to the cantina for our daily afternoon snack of plain crackers and Coca Cola in a glass bottle or in a plastic bag with a straw (nothing too fancy, but always a treat); sending Dad off to work each morning after his question: "What would you like me to bring you when I come home?" And always replying: "Peanuts." Yes, it was that simple – regular shelled peanuts and I'd be beyond thrilled. Maybe I loved the bold, nutty taste or simply the process of cracking them open with my fingers, hearing them snap and carefully putting them in my mouth, keeping them intact, and then trying to do it more quickly than before. I enjoyed eating peanuts and left quite a mess for Mom to clean afterward. And perhaps that was why Dad always brought them home for me, to poke at Mom in the most loving way. There was constant laughter, and a playful energy roamed throughout the house

    I remember walking barefoot around the plaza with my dog, Whitey. He was my protector and friend. We had each other's backs (more like he had mine because he was ferocious enough by himself). I'd go on adventures with other kids–they also loved climbing the big guava tree behind our house, eating the hard, not-quite-ripe-yet fruit. (But I liked them best that way. Far from being sweet and juicy, if anything they were similar to green Anjou pears. I'd sprinkle sea salt on them to intensify the flavor.) We'd put spiders in matchboxes and fight them on little sticks. Rubber bands and playing Jacks were the rave. This was my childhood. For how little we had, I feel so proud of how much good I gained from it.

    We didn't have video games or anything remotely close to that. We enjoyed being outside playing, running, climbing, and exploring. It didn't matter how far we ventured from home, as long as we got back in time for dinner. And dinner was eaten at the table. We'd wash our hands in a bowl of water before diving into the meal (which might have only consisted of rice and fish but was considered a magnificent meal nonetheless). We grew our own livestock and ate whatever we killed or caught that day or what was bought at the market (which someone also had recently caught and killed that morning or the day before). Most of the time (and for me, always), we ate with our hands. And let me tell ya, there's definitely a technique to eating without silverware. It made eating an intimate process. One appreciated food more because you experienced it through the sensation of touch and not just taste or smell.

For children in the Philippines, rain is an exciting experience. And trust me, the rain there is unlike rain in the States. It's like comparing water from one's yard sprinklers to Niagara Falls (okay, maybe not that extreme, but you know what I mean). Kids would run around outside completely clothed, getting drenched as they chased one another, catching frogs, and sometimes using the downpour to take their day's shower. The rain was a bountiful blessing that graced our land, and we welcomed it and indulged in it until, of course, a normal rainstorm became a typhoon, which was not rare where we lived.

Always a scary ordeal, we didn't know whether or not our home would withstand the storm. Anticipating damages not only for us, but for the whole town. Constant flooding occurred every time a typhoon ravaged the area. And as if not frightening enough with thunder, lightning, wind howling in the background, and occasional thuds of things like trees falling to the ground, oftentimes we'd lose electricity. Sitting in candlelight, we couldn't escape the loud, clamoring sounds of rain pounding the tin roof, amplifying the volume of the storm.

"When will this end?" I'd ask my parents.

"I'm not sure. Maybe tomorrow. Maybe in the next couple days. Maybe next week. When the storm is finally exhausted, that's when it will end," my parents would reply.

When the storm eventually moved on, a horrific mess remained, suspending regular daily routines. Homes were destroyed, flooding blocked roads, and debris strewn around town needed to be cleaned up. It wasn't one of those things you walk away from untouched. Our whole world stopped and had to gather itself together, long before any normalcy resumed. Nonetheless, the overall feeling of living in my town was similar to how I imagined Heaven on Earth would feel like.

What I remember most about that old life, even though I was young, was observing true love between my parents. It provided a small glimpse of being in love, to completely admire, be in awe and enthralled with another. They flirted like young lovers in the beginning of a relationship. My father was so romantic, and I could feel my mom was happy and felt safe in his embrace. There was trust and security, support and empowerment. And, most importantly, there was connection beyond anything I can describe in words, so I won't even try.

Sadly, like everything else in this world, this was temporary and met its demise before I could hold onto it and deeply appreciate it for what it was. Dad had a one-way ticket to Saudi Arabia, and Mom and I had one-way tickets to America. Apparently, this had been part of their plan before I'd even shown up; I just happened to prolong the process.

Maybe my subconscious mind has shielded me from remembering that time fully, because the tiny bit that I do recall hurts—it actually hurts. Rushing to get ready to head to the airport for my father's departure is a blur. But two things stand out.

"Stay by us," my mom had said, pointing to a spot near where they sat, holding hands and looking heartbroken.

I squatted down in the middle of the floor in the cold airport. *Hmm. It feels like there's a breeze under my dress. I* looked down. *Oh no! No! I forgot my underwear!* I felt my face get hot. I looked up at my parents. *I'm going to get in trouble...I shouldn't bother them...but I have to tell Mom.*

I leaned over and whispered in my mother's ear, "Mom, I forgot to put on my underwear." I waited for the horrific gasp and a scolding.

"What?" she said. Then let out a big laugh. "It's okay, Grace," she said, probably registering my worried face. She gave me a big hug.

It was embarrassing and humorous, and it broke the tension (quite the needed comic relief), if only for a little bit.

The second thing that left a striking impression: it was probably the first deep wounding of my heart – seeing my parents so sad as they embraced each other, holding back tears (and I'm holding some back as I write this), barely able to speak because of the heaviness of emotions at hand. This, too, was part of love, the heartbreak part. To let go of someone you love so dearly, while unsure of when you'll see that person again, felt like death. That has stayed with me.

After Dad left, Mom and I lingered at home for a few months. There was a low humming vibration in the air that never went away. It reminded us how empty and incomplete life suddenly felt. What a confusing time. I wasn't totally sure what had happened and what was about to occur.

One day we drove back to the city to board this thing called a plane, said to be bigger than any jeepney or bus I had ever been on or seen. And, most importantly, it could fly! My little body had to deal with intense excitement, anxiety, and fear all at once. Up to that point, I'd only known country life - a world where homes had no telephones and often no electricity or power. Unfortunately, where we were going, we'd need to wear shoes daily, and walking out of the house and adventuring by myself at four years old would no longer be allowed.

My fairy tale of a life, simple yet beautiful, became a dream— a goal to achieve again someday. I knew I would; it was just a matter of time. But how ironic that people say America is the land of dreams. In the beginning… it tarnished my own.

Chapter 5

It was quite a rude awakening coming to America. This life, which I thought was perfect and happy, turned upside down like the smile on my face.

We were welcomed with open arms by my mom's large family. I remember walking in, seeing so many unfamiliar faces wanting to greet me. I was scared and wanted to go back to where I came from, but I was nowhere near home. In later weeks, there were parties galore and strangers wanted to hug me and even pick me up, talking to me as if they knew who I was. I struggled, trying to adjust to this new life; I knew my mom did too. As lost and overwhelmed as I felt, she felt the same, on top of being heartbroken and missing Dad, the love of her life. As much as she allowed me to find solace in her embrace, I felt her become distant and preoccupied with transitioning into this new life.

I experienced the contrast between simple country life and the suburbs in good ole' San Diego, which felt like a big city considering where I was from. Stores were huge and filled with more stuff than I had ever seen in my entire life. I remember feeling scared when I'd ride in a car and was buckled in a car seat. I'd wondered: *Why are they tying me down?* Though foreign and unfamiliar, our new lives were cool in that everything had been upgraded, from clothing to buildings, the home we lived in, toys I was now surrounded with, electronics that I had no idea existed.

Gatherings were celebrated with abundant feasts. Tables were filled with familiar food, like pancit and lumpia, and food I had only dreamed of eating someday, like fried chicken. Mom and I were constantly fed pizzas, burgers, fries, milkshakes, and corn dogs, as a means to show off and even win our approval of this new world. Not a bad strategy as I fell in love with those tastes! (It wasn't until we went back home for a visit a couple years later, that I realized how much I missed the taste of freshly picked fruits and veggies and even freshly killed animal in my dish.)

Here, food was packaged and delivered to your closest grocery store and no longer fresh by the time you bit into it. Everything tasted different. Yes, it looked delicious and tasted delicious at first bite, but it didn't make me feel good afterward. This mirrored my new life. Everything looked appealing on the surface. In the depths of my being, I felt a cold hollowness, which I knew was not good for my soul. This feeling underlined the foundation of my life for the next twenty years.

I ached for what lay hidden beyond my false reality—that which was alive and powerful, that which had connection, meaning, and purpose. Was it gone for good? I'd embark on a lifelong adventure to find it again. I don't know how I knew, but I had a feeling and a knowing that I would discover truth to feed my soul with purpose and eventually, life would feel good once more.

Around this time I had my first out-of-body experience. It was early evening and I felt exhausted. As I laid down in the bedroom, I turned on the TV, thinking I could watch a show while I rested. I recall being so tired, that as hard as I tried to stay awake, my eyelids became heavy, and I trailed off to sleep. I woke up shortly. However, looking around I realized I was no longer on the bed, nor was I in my body. I looked down and observed my body sleeping peacefully on the bed while the TV blared in the background along with noise coming from the rest of the house, different conversations happening at once. Although not in the same room, it was as if I were in the middle of it all. Suddenly, an overwhelming feeling filled my entire being, though I couldn't pinpoint what it was.

"I'm small, I know I'm small. But why don't I feel like I

am? I feel huge, not physically, but something about me feels humongous, like I'm part of this thing, this blob-like energy that's filling the room, the whole house."

I didn't know the word at the time, but I felt omnipresent. Like I was a part of this nebulous energy that engulfed the very space of every location my mind could travel to, whether in that room or beyond. The feeling was so strong; I've never forgotten it and unfortunately couldn't describe it in words until now. There was intense contrast between what I was seeing and feeling versus what I thought I knew. I was everywhere and could travel anywhere simply by thought. This was my first experience of this nature and an introduction to the concept of Oneness and God and the fact that there are realms beyond the everyday physical plane.

After that experience, I felt like I was never alone, as if I were forever watched by the invisible. Although there were rumors that our house was haunted, the spirits I had contact with didn't feel like the entities people talked about. Guests and family members who swore they saw apparitions, felt fearful and a sense of negativity during and after their experiences. The first time I saw any kind of spirit with my physical eyes in a waking moment, I felt drawn to it and not at all afraid.

It was Sunday morning, and Mom, along with the rest of my family (grandparents, aunt, and a few uncles), were in the kitchen eating breakfast. I was in my uncle's room playing Nintendo, a room not on the list of where people usually saw these so-called ghosts. I was focused on beating a level, when I suddenly had the feeling I was being watched. I wasn't scared because it felt like I was being watched by a loved one and not an uninvited intruder. One of my relatives must have come into the room, and like anyone else who feels someone's presence, I paused and quickly glanced up. Immediately, I saw a being made of light, and as if that was a normal occurrence, I casually returned to my game.

Wait, what?! What was that?

Instantly I looked back up but it was gone. *Oh my God.* I dropped the controller and ran to the kitchen.

"I just saw something weird, like a person, but made out of light!" I announced to my family.

My uncles laughed and mocked me. "Are you saying that you just saw the ghost that haunts this house? What did she look like? Did you say hi to her? Maybe you should have asked her why she haunts this house! Was she pretty? Maybe next time you should invite her out into the kitchen to show herself to the rest of us."

Okay, they obviously aren't taking me seriously. Of course, they aren't.

"It was light. I'm not sure if it was a woman or not. I don't think it's the ghost you're talking about. I feel it's different. It felt good and not something that wanted to frighten me." *And maybe it doesn't want to show itself to you guys. You might just laugh at it too....*

Mom asked, "How did you feel when you saw it?"

"I felt okay, I guess..."

Grandma butted in, "Oh Grace, you saw the ghost or one of the ghosts that haunts this house. It's made a connection with you. Next time, just kindly ask it to leave you alone."

I didn't feel scared. I don't think it was one of the spirits here. But I guess it could have been. They can't hurt you, right? However if it wanted to hurt me, I would have felt scared, but I didn't. I don't think it was anything bad or evil. I think it was good. And I don't think it's the same ghost they're talking about...

After these experiences, I was convinced there was more to this physical life and a world beyond the veils. But I was not going to subject myself to further ridicule. Dreams of spirit and light beings: ghosts showing me how they died and asking for help, or balls of light giving me instructions and describing a world further away in time than the present – I kept all mystical experiences to myself.

I felt a constant presence lingering around me, and I was

certain more than ever that this was not my imagination. It was Spirit connecting, and I welcomed it because it felt good, not scary or wrong.

For a period of time, my mother attempted to teach me about God and Catholicism, sharing the rosary and other Catholic prayers and bringing me to church with her each week. I was fond of church, but hated going to mass. It felt like a show put on by the people that attended. Families filed in one by one, seemingly put together. After receiving communion, people walked back down the catwalk to their seats, and I could feel their egos shining with excitement as they showed off their Sunday best, hoping to impress the crowd. It bothered me that some kids, forced to act on their best behaviors at church, were still mean at school. During mass the church could feel like sacred ground, but this was dispelled when once I looked up, and a couple girls were giving me and my cousin the evil eye, pointing and laughing at us. The traditional readings felt lifeless. Nothing taught clicked. I always felt there was more than what was shared, that the *entire* truth was held back. My curiosity grew the older I got, which later inspired me to explore outside of religion, which ironically allowed me to deepen my faith.

From the get-go, growing up in the States forced me to be more independent. My mom went to work super early and had a second job afterward. I barely saw her. I sometimes cried in the morning when she left for work. When she woke, I also got up, so we could spend a little time together. I stayed with my grandma and grandpa; in fact, I saw them more than my mom during that time.

There I was, in a foreign land trying to learn a different language and adopt a new way of life. I felt completely out of place.

My mom hardly present, I felt lonely and homesick. I missed my dad. My nights were filled with heartache and hopelessness that I would never feel comfortable in my own surroundings again. During the day, I struggled in school. I couldn't adequately communicate with other students due to the language barrier and culture shock.

Like clockwork, the bell would ring for class to begin, and it was time for my grandpa to walk home. Dread flooded me. I knew I'd have to face six hours of anxiety and embarrassment in the classroom. I'd start to cry, begging him to stay, even though I knew he would leave anyway. The teachers had to carry me off as I sobbed, yelling and flailing my arms, trying to shake their grip off of my body, like a fish caught on the line and whisked out of the water. For about thirty minutes, the teachers would have me sit at one of the tables as I wept. The rest of the class sat on the carpet singing songs and rehearsing nursery rhymes I had never heard of. A repeating refrain went through my young head: *They all seem happy to be here, don't they miss their parents?* As I slowly calmed down, I realized that kids, left and right, were staring at me with looks of disdain and bewilderment. I felt so embarrassed; there was no way of getting out of this one. I was the weird outsider that couldn't communicate. I felt far away from any chance of acceptance.

As weeks passed, I understood that my uncontrollable sobbing in the morning was not going to help me escape school. I joined them on the carpet right after class started. During snack and lunch however, the kids kept their distance. So I kept to myself, usually sitting against a wall watching them play on the playground. I felt like a loser. I was not a part of their universe, just a solitary little planet, alone.

Evenings were no better. I remember sitting by myself trying to complete homework. Filled with anguish and frustration, trying to remember the instructions and what little of them I understood, I longed for my dad or even my mom to help me. I didn't feel comfortable enough to ask for guidance from anybody else. Some of my relatives were also just learning English, and I didn't feel close enough to the rest of them. Seeing my cousin Missy sitting on her dad's lap being read to, getting the exact support I craved, sharpened those painful feelings of isolation.

Although I lived with cousins, after the initial welcome, we didn't grow close. My cousin Missy was only a couple years younger, and although we mostly got along, there seemed to be a disconnect. Partly due to the language barrier, but probably... because of our personalities. A happy kid, she always wanted to play. She was loud and outgoing; I was sad and quiet. Here's a memory which shows what I mean:

A boisterous celebration was in full swing, and in the middle of the party, our mothers took us into the bedroom to dress us exactly alike as if we were twins. We changed into identical dresses, dark red with black polka dots. Excited to be wearing a pretty dress for once, I was eager to finally receive compliments and positive attention. Missy was excited too. She loved getting all prettied up. When we were ready, we were paraded into the room, overflowing with distant family members and family friends I hadn't met yet. Instantly I felt self-conscious. I'm not even sure I smiled. I hated being in a crowd of strangers and felt myself wince in embarrassment, wanting to hide. Missy on the other hand, self-assured, easily accepted the praise. It felt as if everyone was fawning over her while I stood there awkwardly, *barely* receiving any attention, let alone compliments. It dawned on me that I was an outsider, even among my own family. My mother, being shy herself, played it off like it went well. I assume they were unaware of how insecure I was feeling and had no idea how much extra kindness I needed.

When we muster the courage to heal ourselves, the first place we must venture is back to early family life. What happened to us then that formed walls within our hearts? What may have happened to that little girl's self-confidence if a few family members had understood her shyness and treated her tenderly? Now, as adults, we have to reconnect with that hurt child and offer her compassion and tenderness ourselves. For as you'll see... the road to repair is steep and long.

Chapter 6

Solitude. What seemed like a prickly family situation (likely due to my low self-esteem), pushed me to accept this state. Gradually, being alone became comforting the more I embraced it. I learned to be an observer, since in the beginning, I didn't know how to speak English. It forced me to pay attention to everyone's actions and the way they spoke. Most importantly, I learned to understand what they were really saying by sensing the emotions of the person speaking. I got a lot more out of this practice than one would gain by merely listening to words. It became clear that, at times, people's energies were different from how they portrayed themselves through language. I noticed that people often hid behind walls, rarely allowing their real selves to be seen.

A surprising gift emerged from feeling alone and conversing in my head: I learned how to pray- or what I thought was prayer, which was really just another conversation I had in my head, but with God. I spoke to whom I believed was God and anyone else in the heavens who would spare me a moment.

My conversations usually sounded like this: "Hi again, God. I know you're listening, so please help me escape this world. I know I've already asked a handful of times this week, but I figured it was worth another try. I'll probably ask you again tomorrow. Also, please let Mom come home early tonight so I can see her before I fall asleep. And please take care of Dad. He's alone where he is, without me or Mom. And oh yeah, send me a cat, too, while you're at it. They won't let me have a dog here. Today, I almost remembered the word "fork" in ESL… Oh hey, look at that, I remembered it…"

The more I did this, the more natural it was to talk to the invisible. I felt like someone was actually listening. This little practice comforted me. And in no time, this man started showing up in my dreams and in my mind whenever I closed my eyes—I later learned in church and in CCD (Catechism class) that he fit the description of the man they called the Son of God, Jesus. So I started calling him Jesus, and He became my invisible friend, constantly showing up in nocturnal visits and in my mind's eye whenever I prayed, meditated, or felt alone. This was part of what saved me from utter loneliness growing up. And it strengthened my faith, my ability to continue believing in something greater than what I knew of myself and my present reality.

I talked to this man, Jesus, about everything, and I mean *everything*. We spoke every day, and when I prayed at night, it was always to Him. Often, I even laughed with Him, like He was a real friend in the physical world. He was down to earth but with divine-like attributes, radiating a modest aura of divinity. There wasn't pomp and circumstance you'd expect when meeting Him, but you simply knew it was Him. He was funny and cracked me up with jokes. He was so much more than the Jesus that The Bible and church described. Human, like it was easy being with Him –no pressure or expectations to be a certain way or to be "perfect." He accepted me as I was.

And the dreams! He talked to me of life beyond the physical, gave me instructions, told me things regarding myself, and taught me what life was about: love. Even at a young age, I understood this because I felt it with my heart, separate from logically piecing it together in my mind. It was a relief to be respected and have my spiritual inquires responded to. When I asked questions in Catechism class (I was curious and inspired to explore deeper), I'd get in trouble.

"Oh Grace, there's nothing else to the parable. We talked

about what it means, and that's that. Jesus is the way, and only Him. Don't you want to join the rest of the class outside for a snack?"

I even got into an argument with a facilitator at confirmation camp, posing questions I guess he didn't want to contemplate or answer. Such as:

"Don't you feel maybe there's more to the stories about Jesus than we're told? How do we know that the people who wrote these books in The Bible didn't exaggerate, create, leave out, or misinterpret any of these teachings? What parts of these teachings are similar to other religions and beliefs? Why is it so bad to try to create a commonality between different beliefs? Maybe they're all talking about the same thing?"

I argued that maybe we needed to look at religion from different perspectives and expand our minds to expand our understanding of truth. But here was the response:

"How dare you question the church and its teachings? The Bible is a collection of divine writings designated by the church as the word of God. Other perspectives aren't needed because The Bible provides the answers. You questioning and exploring different beliefs indicates that you lack faith."

Whether or not he understood my queries, he was a defender of the church, and nothing I could say or do gained acceptance for my stance, especially once I realized it wasn't about winning or losing the argument. For me, it was merely an attempt to shed more light and gain more understanding of the real truth...wherever it could be found.

That facilitator became a priest later on in life. I respect him for defending his church, his religion, and his God. But I really just wanted to know more.

Every time I felt sad, and there were lots of those times, I'd roll into a ball in the corner of my bed and cry.

Damn you, Jesus, where the hell are you? Why aren't You here with me in physical and tangible form? I'm in so much pain. Why do You allow me to suffer alone? So much for being my Savior...

Every time I felt this despondent, even from when I was ten years old, something phenomenal happened. As I closed my crying eyes, a vision would take over my entire reality. Within my mind, I saw Jesus approach me, His whole being emanating with an energy of peace and love. "It's going to be okay," He'd say. "You don't have to feel sad anymore. Let go, you can let go anytime you want."And as I released the grief, breathing out a big sigh of relief, He and I floated upwards until our surroundings were no longer that of Earth. Wherever He took me, the place was bright and the energy of peace filled the space. He'd invite me to sit with Him at a table where we feasted on delicious food unlike anything I had ever seen or tasted. It was like consuming air, extremely light, however I knew that it tasted delicious and filled me just enough. We would laugh throughout the meal, and I magically forgot about whatever it was I was sad about beforehand.

After a while, a big tree showed up in the vision. *Why is this here?* I tried to make it disappear, but couldn't erase it! *What's going on?* After all, *I* was creating that vision, or so I thought. But Jesus explained that the tree had meaning and I'd understand why it was there someday. (I learned about the Tree of Life in my twenties. Everything it stood for explained why it had shown up in my visions. Its roots became thicker and stronger, digging deeper into the ground as it stood taller and larger, the older I got. It aged as I aged. That tree, was my tree of life, representing me.)

My relationship with Jesus also deepened and grew stronger over time. I still attended mass at this point but it was pretty much a weekly routine that I carelessly participated in. Outside of church, my spiritual sagacity grew. I learned about life on a deeper level and more about faith on a soul level than when I was in the presence of dogma and religion. The things I felt and my interactions with Jesus were catalysts for greater insight about life and God – wisdom.

I can't quite put it into words, but I always felt like I was *home* every time I closed my eyes and connected to Spirit, connected to God. Although it made me yearn to *go home,* to a place I knew was not on Earth, this oddly provided solace and pumped a little more life into me.

At such a young age, I couldn't convey any of this to others – this grand thing I was experiencing: an invisible world beyond the one we were blindly living in. And though part of me thrived as I developed this rich, inner world, I felt different, and wanted desperately to fit in. At surface level, I worked hard to do so. Starting school and finally speaking English, I gradually got there. I created relationships with my cousins and made friends with kids at school. I even became a class leader in fact, being a part of student government from early on in elementary school. I met my best friend, Samaira, who continued to act like a sister throughout my life. She'd weave in and out over the years but never disappeared for too long. She was wise on a deeper level than other kids at school. On the outside, she is sweet, soft-spoken, yet extremely funny and cracked jokes all the time. Everyone loved her. But in private, we talked about our perspectives on life that expanded further and deeper than things we talked about with other kids. She got things and knew things. I could tell that she felt people and things like I did. This gave me a safe space to revel in for a small moment or two while at school. And her voice, there were so many times she sang to me when I was feeling down. And as beautiful as her voice was, it was one of the treasures she kept hidden from the world. I know for sure that she and I have been soul mates for many lifetimes before this one.

Needless to say, my world became a little warmer and not as lonely. Finally I was having fun and playing! And I think a part of me did my best to forget about my old life in order to live comfortably on the surface level without the burden of knowing that life could offer more. I allowed myself to settle for the time being. However, in my alone time, I continued to be introspective and thought deeply about the magical world separate from the physical. This still hurt at times, but not as much as it once had. I still desperately wanted to go *home*, wherever *home* was. The conversations I shared with Jesus became robust and filled with so much more depth, but also incorporated more laughter and human verity.

"Okay, so I have a crush on this guy, Michael Bass, at school."

"Ohhhhh I know. I helped you write that love letter to him, remember?" He laughed as He pointed out how He knew all this time...

"Hey, don't laugh! And really, can you just not be in my head sometimes. I mean, just don't go there when I'm thinking about Mike, okay?"

"I'm always with you, don't you know this?"

"Yeah, yeah, yeah... I know, you *always* know."

"Of course I always know. I Am always with you. We are One. You and I are of the same essence that make up the other."

"But You're the Son of God, Christ, the Lord... how can we possibly be the same? I'm just Grace."

"You are all of that, too. It's in your name, Divine Grace."

I felt grateful to have my relationship with Jesus, and living in the States became a bit more bearable. I thought the sharp edges of discomfort from assimilating to a new world had been filed down. Unfortunately, separation from those we love creates an emptiness which will not be denied.

Chapter 7

Papa, I miss you, when am I going to see you again?

I missed my dad dearly. Back then, because calling long distance was tough on the wallet, we barely spoke.

It took my mom a handful of times to get the call through.

"Grace hurry, come here now, it's ringing! We don't have much time," Mom would excitedly yell from across the room.

I quickly dropped whatever I was doing.

"Papa! Papa! Pa, I miss you so much. I love you. What are you doing there?"

"Ah Grace, I miss you, too, anak! I love you!"

"Is it nighttime there or is it daytime?"

"It's morning here. I just woke up in time to talk to you!"

"Pa, I'm finally learning how to read! Can you write to me too, separately from your letters to Mom?"

"Oh, is that right?! Yes of course! I'm so proud of you. Keep it up, nak'! Did you see that one episode on Full House the other day when Stephanie almost loses Mr. Bear?"

"Hahaha, yes Dad I saw that! That's so cool that you watch Full House too! Ahh, okay, okay, Pa, I have to give it to Mama now before we need to go. I love you, Papa. I miss you so much."

"I love you too, nak'! I miss you so much! I cry every time I think of you…"

"Me too, Pa…"

I hated having a rushed conversation every time we spoke on the phone, but I enjoyed hearing his voice. At times, his voice would crack mid-sentence, and he'd have to gather himself real quick before he'd start crying. It would be a waste to cry on the phone since we had so little time to talk. It was frustrating, missing my dad. I wanted to hear his voice, but every time we got off the phone, it emphasized how much I missed him.

Sometimes, out of nowhere, sadness because of being apart struck me, and a pool of tears would stream down my face. Rushing to my room and pulling out my collection of his old handkerchiefs, I'd hold them to my chest, sobbing and calling out to him. I'd crush them into my nose, trying to smell any lingering scent. After a while, I dressed my life-size teddy bear in one of his old shirts. Holding on to it, I'd lay in bed pretending it was Dad's chest I was crying into. I can't emphasize enough how much it hurt missing my dad, how frustrating not to be able to talk to him whenever I wanted. I wished so much to go back to the home we all shared, the things about that life that made it spectacular. I missed sharing meals with him, goofing around, and giving Mom a hard time in a sort of loving way with him.

It was like a chant from my heart: *I miss our rocking chair. I miss our old house where that rocking chair sitting, collecting dust. I miss Dad. I miss Mom, even though she's with me; I hardly get to be with her. I miss our old life, so much.*

And plunging into sorrow felt like death, unfortunately, too often.

I was then introduced to the art of writing love letters — the most affordable way to communicate with Dad. He wrote love letters to Mom and like he said he would, to me. We excitedly wrote back, signing off with I love you's and kisses. I wrote him a few pages at times, describing experiences at school, what I was learning, home-life with Mom's family, and recent episodes of Full House. Dad made sure he was up-to-date on Full House, not missing a show on his end, knowing I would question him about it. I looked forward to running and getting the mail in hopes there would be a letter from Dad. Sometimes weeks went by when we wouldn't receive anything, but without fail, I always ran to the mailbox when I knew the mailman had come by.

Besides writing letters, this unfortunate situation inspired Mom and me to become more creative in how we communicated with Dad. We recorded ourselves on cassette tapes, talking as if conversing in real time with each other. I played them over and over, capturing every detail of his voice, the emotions behind his words. I could feel his energy!

For seven long, grueling years, Dad lived apart from us. We saw him only twice and only for about a month's time each visit. The first time, we met back in the Philippines for my parents' wedding. I was their flower girl. I was six years old and we'd been gone for about a year and a half. Dad looked leaner than I remembered. And although we hadn't been away that long, I remember feeling like a foreigner in my old home. I wasn't used to certain things anymore. I remember visiting Dad's family's house on the other end of town from where we were staying at Mom's family's place. I was not looking forward to the long walk ahead, travelling on the dirt road, through the woods. There were no street lights. When it got dark, I didn't realize how dark it really got! But Dad knew his way and wasn't afraid. He had been walking through these woods and on these dirt roads since he was a kid.

It was August, so it was rainy season. And oh my, did I forget how strong and powerful the rain was back there. But I remembered how exciting it was for kids in town when it rained. Like old times, I jumped in puddles and got soaked as I played with kids in the plaza. It was total freedom once again. I wandered off as I pleased, adventuring with kids I used to play with.

The food was incredible! I forgot how delicious it was to eat fresh- fresh anything! The fish and the freshly killed pig, the veggies grown from outside our house, and the different types of fruits I would never find in the States- it was like heaven! I couldn't get enough to eat! Every dish, though simple and not fancy at all, was better than the food I consumed on a daily basis back in the States. No cheeseburger compared to rice and a Filipino dish that consisted of freshly killed meat and veggies. As before, because it wasn't frowned upon like it was back in the States, I ate with my hands at every meal. I was home, and it felt good.

Family from all over gathered to attend Mom and Dad's wedding. I was forced to wake up early that warm morning. The house was already filled with crowds of people getting the house ready for a feast after the ceremony. Relatives were cooking with huge pots and pans in the kitchen outside, some started to get dressed themselves, while the rest watched as Mom got dolled up before slipping into her white dress. I was surprised how extravagant her dress was. I always thought Mom was a simple lady, but not that day. It was her big day, so she went big altogether — her dress, hair, and everything from the crowd that joined us in celebration to the smile she wore all day long.

That was probably one of the happiest days of my life, as I watched Mom and Dad promise one another their love. If only I could re-live that moment.

The second time we visited with my father was probably the happiest time of my adolescent life. We travelled back to the Philippines with my mom's whole family for a full month's vacation. Being a little older, I took in how incredibly romantic my parents were in each other's presence. I must have taken a thousand pictures of them with my mind and my heart as they canoodled at every opportunity. They were the happiest they had ever looked. Everything felt right. I didn't want it to end as I anxiously heard the clock ticking louder and louder in the back of my mind as this beautiful and yet ephemeral moment slowly slipped into the past.

With it went the innocence of my early life in the Philippines. However, I realized that the person I was becoming was growing beyond that physical place, and ultimately it became a romanticized idea of life—a fantasy. That was the last time I traveled back to my first home. When I said goodbye, I knew it would be a long while before I returned.

(And I haven't made it back yet. I'm not sure I'd fit in if I did. I've changed, and the quaint little town has evolved as well. Now it boasts paved roads; houses are built stronger and bigger to battle annual typhoons; people have televisions and various kinds of electronics; and like the rest of the world, they carry around cell phones, go on Facebook, and chat with family overseas. So much for the simple life I remember, it's not quite the same these days.)

Ironically, the marriage of my parents (which I had joyously celebrated), precipitated an unforeseen insecurity. Maybe since being a teen is such a chaotic time of figuring out who one is, even something symbolic can rock one's sense of steady grounding. Surprisingly, feelings of being outside the nuclear circle sprouted – because my mother and father shared the same last name, but I still carried my grandfather's. This whole identity thing was a crisis – not only in my physical world, but deep within my soul. Literally and spiritually speaking, who was I? I felt lost; my identity didn't match who I really was.

And to add a seismic shift to the family, Mom had become pregnant after that last visit. Nine months later, I stood in the labor room and watched my little sister being born. It was a pretty incredible experience, especially at nine and a half years old. If my parents had ever wanted to subtly introduce me to the idea of birth control, that was the perfect moment. However, looking back, I'm glad I was there. I saw the world welcome my baby sister as she came out crying, covered in blood, and breathing in this thing called Life. I definitely feel that was the most magical moment I had witnessed so far.

As soon as baby Donna arrived, I became her second mom. I woke up in the middle of the night and helped changed her. I learned to make milk at two o'clock in the morning, learned to put her to sleep, and, really, learned to love another soul that was dependent on me. I watched her when my mom left early for work and after school. I learned to become a parent at quite a young age. But I enjoyed it. While everyone else was talking about crushes at school, who kissed whom, and other mindless juvenile things, I was helping parent my little sister. But she brought me so much joy. I was no longer an only child! My prayers were finally answered, and I was no longer alone. But as there's usually a downside to every event, at times, when parts of me wanted to be a kid, I resented this. It stripped me of a childhood too early. I was responsible not just for myself, but for another soul. That's too much pressure when you're only nine!

A year and a half later, Dad finally moved to the States. And shortly after, my baby brother decided to join the picture. I was a big sister to two little munchkins, for whom I continued to play the role of second mom.

Our family was whole and complete, but a discomfort jabbed at me from somewhere deep. Everyone in the household but me shared the same last name. I loved my grandfather, but I was my dad's daughter, and I wanted my last name to match everyone else's in the family.

"Mom, you now carry Dad's last name, and so do Donna and Mark. Why can't I change mine? Aren't I Dad's daughter too? Don't I have the right to use his name if I want to?"

"Yes, you are your father's daughter. But because of the way we prepared your papers when coming to America, we used my maiden name because your Dad and I weren't married. And with all your legal paperwork still showing that name and you still being a legal resident and not a U.S. citizen yet, we aren't able to change your name until you become a naturalized citizen. And for some reason, when I became a citizen, you didn't automatically become one like we thought you would, as a minor under me. But wait a few more years, and when you're 18 years old, you'll go through the citizenship process, take the test, and finally be sworn in as a U.S. citizen. Then you can change your last name. That would be the easiest way to go about it. So make sure you pay attention in U.S. History class, you'll need all that information to pass the citizenship test!"

I was left without a choice but to be patient and wait for the time when I could finally change my last name and feel like I belonged to my family. I'll never know if that would have centered me or reduced the tumultuous years around the corner. But if I had to hint at what was to come…an emotional typhoon just about sums it up.

Chapter 8

As I approached my early teen years, I wanted to be more in the physical world and less in my mind, less introspective, barely even praying. I tried so hard to fit in, but the more effort I put out, the less successful I was. I was creating an image far from who I truly was. And almost every night, I cried about this. I shared a room with two of my young uncles, since we were still living at my grandma's house. This made it awkward at night. I knew they heard me trying to silently cry myself to sleep. But no one brought it up.

It didn't help that these were the years of hellish puberty, of hormones causing havoc on multiple levels of my being. So as much as I wanted to be a different type of person – more extroverted and superficial, like my peers, no matter how I avoided my true self, at every emotional breakdown, I naturally turned inward toward what had proven to be safe for so many years: prayer and what I later recognized as meditation.

The war between the outer world and my inner sacred space worsened during high school. After a few years of saving money, Dad bought a home for our family, and we were finally able to move out of my mother's family's house. It was a small place, a 900 square-foot condo with two bedrooms, but it was enough for us. Although I shared a room with my sister and brother, in the beginning, they slept in my parents' room which afforded me the privacy I had craved for so long. I wept at night as much as I wanted without worrying about making too much noise. I prayed and cried myself to sleep so many nights thinking, *I just want to go home, wherever that may be* (but I hoped it wasn't on this physical plane).

Building a false image took a toll on me. I smiled and seemed fine, but inside I lacked self-love and the will to thrive in the outside world.

I went to school and acted according to what I thought was normal; when I'd come home, I'd retreat into my cave, embarking on a never-ending journey to find purpose. I couldn't understand why life still felt incomplete even though my family was whole and under one roof- our own roof. Maybe it was because I saw the distance between Mom and Dad growing. They, too, were stuck under pressures of life, robotically living on this surface level. Where was the depth we had shared? The energy between us seemed fake and cold, and I loathed this superficial existence. It definitely was not good enough, and I certainly didn't feel like I was good enough for *it*.

Most of the time I felt judged – so much pressure to be perfect, smart, and good. Ignorance is bliss, they say, and maybe if I hadn't been aware that life had potential to be more than what I was experiencing, I wouldn't have felt so discontented and miserable with what I had. How could I feel accepted when the good I did was overlooked, but the smallest mistake or imperfection was examined under a microscope. I didn't think this was fair.

Regularly, I'd overhear my mom spread news of my latest transgression to her sister. One instance comes to mind: "Grace snuck out last night. She climbed out of her bedroom window and made Missy lie about her whereabouts to us. We got a call from the police station around one o'clock. I guess her friend was driving his sister's new car. The cops took them all in, realizing they were teens that had snuck out past curfew, and they didn't have the proper licenses or permits to even be driving!"

Great, the whole family will be talking about me in a couple hours' time. She makes me sound like a horrible kid. And maybe I am because I snuck out but I never get to do anything with my friends.

"Okay, so I snuck out, yes, that was bad," I said to my mother. "But my friends and I weren't doing anything wrong. I was helping them send love letters to their significant others in the middle of the night. And you and Dad never allow me out. How does this make me a bad person? The whole family thinks I'm such a rebellious kid. But you keep me caged up like a prisoner."

"You could have gotten hurt," Mom said. "Something could have happened, you never know. It's not safe driving around in the middle of the night. You snuck out and lied about it and made your cousin lie about it too. All of this is wrong and bad."

"So you guys choose this to be the one thing you talk to the family about regarding me? What about all the other times I actually excelled in school considering where I came from? Don't you remember? I've never gotten help on homework from you or anyone…and I couldn't even speak English when I started school! I taught myself to read and write while struggling to speak this complicated language. You or Dad, never once sat and read with me, no one ever did."

"Oh, but you know why we couldn't. I didn't know the language either. And your dad was away. Why can't you just accept all this? It's not like we did it to intentionally hurt you."

"I understand, I really do. But it still hurts and it still happened, and I don't get why that's not talked about with the family instead- how independent I was and continue to be. I was the outsider in school because I was a foreigner, but a couple years later, what do you know, I step into a leadership position. Was any of that talked about? No!"

"And you know, I'm really proud of you for that…"

"That's not the point, Mom. You don't tell anyone else in the family about my success."

"Because I don't have to. As long as you know I'm proud of you, I don't have to tell anyone else."

"Why not? Why only the "bad" stuff, that normal teenagers do? I wanted to do extracurricular activities outside of school, but we didn't have enough money. So I came out looking like I had no talent because I didn't take up something like piano or any sports. And now, I go out on long runs on my own because I want to, because I get a little peace from it, for crying out loud, not because I'm part of a team or because I have to do it. I've taught myself to play the guitar (which I bought for myself), and even write songs. I know how to clean the house; if you gave any of my cousins a broom and a duster, they wouldn't even know where to start."

Mom started chuckling. "Yes, that's true. They wouldn't even know where to start…"

"Yeah, exactly! I helped you raise Donna and Mark. I woke up in the middle of the night with you numerous times, lost sleep with you, tirelessly kept going so it would be a little easier for you. Where is all this in your conversations with the family?"

"You know I appreciate all your help when it comes to your brother and sister, I always have. But there's no need to talk about those things. You need to stay humble in *everything* you do with everyone you meet. You pray to Jesus, don't you? So then you know that humility is important in staying aligned with His teachings."

Shame on me for not being perfect, because those times of imperfection were definitely more worth speaking about. What an incredibly backward kind of thinking. Was acknowledging one's strengths not taught back then?

"Mom, I'm the goddamn class president of my high school class; I'm maintaining good grades, challenging myself with honors and AP classes, exploring different colleges in the hope to attend one of them. I work on weekends so I don't have to ask you to pay for things. I don't even go out with my friends. I don't party and hang out with people. I watch my siblings all the time and help them with homework. I clean the house with you on weekends, and my bed is *always* made before I even walk out of my room in the morning. I don't really ask for anything."

"And that's why I am so proud of you. For having the

drive to go forth in becoming successful on your own."

"But I still don't get why you and the rest of the family don't see my efforts. I'm never recognized. But God forbid, when I actually do hang out with the kids in our neighborhood past 7pm, I'm such a bad kid."

"Because that is a distraction. You need to stay focused."

"How much more focused could I be! Maybe when I speak my mind because I don't agree with the wrong that I see in our family, I'm suddenly a horrible person. Don't you know that when I'm in my room, I'm usually praying? I don't ever ask you to drive me to the movies or to the mall with friends. I ask you to drive me to church. I just don't get where I'm getting all this wrong? Why would you tell the family everything I do that's wrong and not anything else about me, like my accomplishments?"

"Boasting isn't what we do in this family. It's not humble. I'm proud of you, of what you have done and continue to do, but I don't have to tell everyone that. If you keep doing good things, people will automatically see it. You won't have to tell them because they'll already see."

It didn't work out like that. My efforts were unseen, and my imperfections always took the spotlight. I didn't believe I was anything special because I was never recognized or let alone, acknowledged, but God, I knew there was so much more of me they didn't see or care to learn about—perhaps something that would make the cut of being *enough*. It hurt me to the core that they made no effort to know the real me. I spoke up a lot. I was never the kind to not speak my truth. And for this, I got in trouble. Being strong-willed and outspoken was part of what made me a "bad" child, I suppose.

The way I was talked about and treated, had me believing I was worthless, ugly, talentless, unintelligent, unkind, selfish, cold, and pretty much a horrible kid. They would have known I was full of life, of love, if they had given me a chance to be me and allowed me to feel safe speaking freely (a situation everyone would flourish in!).

I took up running to get out of the house, escape its lifeless energy and be by myself to talk with Jesus and God, beyond my bedroom walls. Sometimes the conversations consisted of pleas for help, or angry words aimed at them. I railed, *Why am I still here? I don't want to be here.* I felt utterly unhappy. Wasn't I too young to be thinking like that and feeling this sad for so long? I wanted something more, but most teenagers don't know how to mobilize their energies for productive endeavors. I was no different. Instead, what was accessible was the desire to disappear from this place forever.

As I went further into my teenage years, I watched Dad become more aggravated and angry at life and even at me. Our relationship deteriorated. What a loss; he was no longer the dad I remembered. Our home was tense. Constantly fearful, we lived on high alert to make sure not to trigger his temper, a dark cloud hanging over us. No one wanted to instigate a surprise lightning strike when he was around. Mom grew quiet and took less initiative. My siblings looked to me for something, anything, but at that point, my only strategy was to close my bedroom door and journal as I cried or went into prayer or meditation.

I appeared highly functional, did well in school, worked part time here and there, enjoyed time alone, went on long runs. I screwed on a smile and acted like nothing bothered me; life was just peachy. Deep down, I was a mess. I didn't feel like I belonged. I felt criticized by the people who filled my world. What they saw was the surface, not the person I truly was inside.

Could I really blame them? I kept that person hidden, and pretty much kept to myself. I didn't go to parties and wasn't allowed to hang out with friends outside of school except for some of my neighbors (who became life-long friends), with an early curfew. I don't think I was a bad kid. But Dad was overly strict, and anything that seemed opposite of his will was impermissible. How could I breathe growing up like that?

Chapter 9

I don't know to what depths I would have sunk if not for this insistent spiritual calling. I'd ask Mom to bring me to church when there was no mass so I could sit quietly in prayer by myself. And I was lucky that I liked to write in my journal because I penned off endless letters to God -about my recurrent dreams. They'd started before my teen years, mysterious and chock full of entities that were not of this physical world. I wanted answers from God.

    I dreamt of being chased near my grandmother's house (where I had spent most of my adolescent years). The same entity chased every time, though I could never make out what it was. It was a scary dream. Not knowing what was running after me, but feeling like it was huge and if it caught me, that'd be the end of me. I could tell it was an entity of some sort, something not belonging in the physical world. I always got away in the end, but the dream seemed real. I'd wake up gasping for air, as if I'd actually been running in real life, relieved it was only a dream.

    Other nocturnal journeys featured what seemed to be spirits in grandma's house. They wanted to tell or show me something. I couldn't understand why. Was it because I was the only one who would pay attention and listen intently? Each time I'd attempt to follow them to a place beyond the boundaries of the house, something tugged at me to stop, and I'd wake up. I never felt afraid, just curious and wanted to explore further. Who were these spirits? Obviously, they were no longer living and appeared stuck in the in-between. One dream in particular, felt like I had woken up in an alternate Universe or different dimension, though present time. I found myself in one of the bedrooms dimly lit by one candle which my mom held as she approached me.

"Don't forget to make a wish at the end," she quietly said in a rather creepy voice.

"Wait what?! A wish?! Why aren't the lights on, and why are you holding a candle?" I responded.

Instantly she disappeared. My attention went to the master bedroom door that slowly opened to the hallway, also dimly lit. As I stepped outside of the bedroom, immediately to my left, my dead aunt floated by, dressed in back. I had never met her in real life, but recognized her from photographs. Right behind her, two little girls played a clapping-hand game. They were in black and white unlike the rest of the scene and in moving in slow motion like an old movie. I heard them talk and giggle as it echoed in the background as if they were far away. I could tell they were from the 1940's from their outfits: dresses with big bows in the front and similar bows in their hair. And lastly, after they glided out of the room, there was a baby boy, crawling. He was no more than 10 months old, wearing a blue onesie. And although it looked like a baby, I got the impression that he was old; his spirit mirrored that of an adult man. As I watched them float into the hallway, following my dead aunt, the hallway stretched out longer and longer. The end was pitch black. The baby looked back at me, as if to motion me to follow. Right away, my body floated on ahead until I reached my dead aunt's side. I gazed up at her as she slowly turned her head to look at me. She was beautiful, exactly as family had described her. She leaned over and whispered into my ear. For the life of me, I can't remember what she said, but it must have been important from the way she grinned at me afterwards. As if telepathically communicating, I heard her tell me not to forget. Her mouth never moved. *What is it that I'm not supposed to forget?*

I had no time to think or ask her to explain because the closet door to the right of me creaked opened. It was pitch black. Was a whole new universe in there or a portal that led to one? As my aunt started to enter, she looked back at me, as if instructing me to follow. One by one, they walked into the closet and disappeared. I started to head into the blackness, when I felt someone pull me back from behind, keeping me from entering all the way.

Suddenly, I was running down my grandma's street like in my other reoccurring dream. In a second's time, I was back in her house, but in the darkened master bedroom, where the ghosts initially came from, and where hauntings were usually experienced by guests. While I became aware of where I was, I realized that my grandma was walking towards me with the same candle my mom had held in the beginning of the dream. And even before I could ask questions, she said, "Did you make a wish? I hope you did…" And boom, I awoke.

I woke up not knowing what to think. It was such an eerie dream but I wasn't frightened, just curious and wanted to learn more. I immediately looked for pictures of my dead aunt in albums. And sure enough, she looked exactly the way she did in my dream. As much as we had crazy experiences in that house, whether seeing apparitions or hearing children playing or a baby crying, we never thought to bless it or hold a séance to get rid of these stuck energies.

Apart from dreams of entities chasing after me and dead people wanting to talk to me, I dreamt of light beings. They looked like balls of light or simply light that gave me instructions about life and showed me visions of an ancient world and a future world (dependent on how well mankind took care of its present one). Visions emphasized the collaboration with mankind as a whole. Humanity working together and what that would produce in this world. I also was shown the consequences if we continued to draw borders between one another. From a world filled with desolate and lifeless places like that of a barren desert, to a world lush and full of life, its entirety encapsulated by peace and love. They told me there once was a time when our world thrived in perfection, and little by little, discord created by human beings slowly made its negative impact. But there were hopeful messages: that we could recreate that kind of world, perfect and harmonious, but a lot of effort and work had to be put forth to help us achieve that.

My dreams were mysteries, but I believed they opened the door to a Universe more vast and meaningful than the one I was living in. This confirmed that there was life beyond this place and that God existed, along with Spirit, somewhere in the ethers, aiding humanity and those awake and aware enough to pay attention to their call. And the more I felt connected to that truth, the more I wanted to help people experience the sacredness of that connection, due to the love and peace it provided.

I stumbled over the topic of St. Therese, the Little Flower. I was so intrigued by her story, I started praying her novenas. At the early age of fifteen, she had become a nun, the youngest Carmelite sister to date. I wanted to be like her and felt her story resonated with mine. St. Therese, like me, had a strong relationship with Jesus and was always in prayer. Even though she was sickly since childhood and had moments that tremendously challenged her throughout her life, she never lost faith nor did it shake her connection with God. She believed in "the little way" and in doing things with great love as a way to get to heaven. Her approach to faith was through simple acts of kindness and focus on doing ordinary things with great love. This intensified my desire to share my own closeness with Jesus and help people feel that majestic love and care that results from connecting with Source.

As a child, my mom had made friends with a few ladies that she said were intuitive who had a special connection with God. Upon meeting them, they had told me that I would someday be doing God's work (which sounded extremely unspecific). Perhaps the time was coming when I'd fulfill what they had meant. Yes! I could be a nun, spreading Love into the world. I was totally pumped. I wanted people to not feel afraid of what existed beyond this surface life—beyond the veils. A life doing God's work through the church would afford me freedom from intense loneliness at home, and I was passionate about Spirit and saving others from their own sadness and hurt. If I could save the world, I would save myself, which was wrong thinking. I needed to save myself first. Regardless, I was set on being a nun at fourteen years old.

Around this time, my dreams intensified. Jesus came to me in the middle of the night and told me to follow him so he could show me something. But every time I tried to follow, something pulled me back, and I'd awake. The dreams where Spirit would speak with me continued as well but felt more vivid and real. Those in which I was chased came more often. The intensity of my internal spiritual world was palpable. Sadly, I had no one to speak with about this. All I had was prayer. So it made sense to become a nun – the perfect way to alleviate fears, put me under a holy light of protection, right? Little did I know, that wasn't the case. For starters, I was already protected by light, as we all are, and second, my reason to go into the nun-hood should have been solely to do God's work and help the world, not escape it. I hadn't tapped into that wisdom yet. As I processed these ideas, high school life seemed boring and bland. I disengaged. I pretended to be interested in the silly things teenage girls find so amusing, but in reality, I was completely disinterested to the point that it exhausted me to live day after day in such a fake world.

Eager and excited to chart a new life course, I approached my CCD teacher. I was positive I'd get her support. Fortunately, I got something better.

"I've been wanting to talk to you about an idea I've become enamored with lately. Have you heard of St. Therese, The Little Flower?" I asked her.

"Yes, of course I know who she is. She's one of my favorite saints," she responded.

"Yes- mine too! And well, I want to be like her. I want to

be a nun just like her. I want to share my faith and the love I have for Jesus and God with people. I want to share the message of love with people! I'm so excited! What do you think?"

"Well, dear, I think that's wonderful that you have this great admiration for St. Therese. She's an admirable saint to adore and have as a role model, however, I would rethink becoming a nun."

"Really? But I want to do God's work and help spread the message of love and faith throughout the world. What better way to do that than by being a nun?"

"Sweetheart, you'd only be held back from your mission of sharing such beautiful messages if you became a nun. There are politics and so many rules that you'd need to abide by that could potentially keep you from truly doing what you wanted to do," she explained.

She stopped me in my tracks and helped me gain perspective on the real reasons why I wanted to pursue that path. It was mostly to escape. And although I also sincerely wanted to do God's work and help the world, she revealed that being a nun would, unfortunately, limit my ability to do that! Considering the red tape that came with being a nun, I wouldn't have the total freedom I'd need to share Love with the world in the manner I wanted to.

This made her the best person I could have approached. Believe it or not, my CCD teacher inspired me to release the idea of becoming a nun. It was at that same time that I noticed a shift in my understanding of what God meant in the religion. The explanation I had been given didn't sit well with me. Wasn't God supposed to be Love, and isn't Love supposed to be freeing? Why didn't I feel that from what I had learned? Instead, I had been directed to focus on a ton of guilt and condemnation that my religion generously dished out. I didn't feel safe to be me without judgment; if anything, I felt worse as a person. I knew I wanted to do God's work, which translated, in my mind, to offering pure, good actions to the world - sharing the love I felt whenever I connected to God, to

Source. I realized my motives no longer aligned with the religion I had been taught

I abandoned religion and deemed myself "spiritual." I continued practicing certain Catholic traditions- praying the rosary because I believed in that prayer (and others), but no longer identified as a "Catholic." It's not that I didn't believe in God; if anything I believed *more* deeply in that concept, as well as the idea of life beyond this plane. My relationship with Jesus also strengthened. I would have to say my faith saved my life time and time again.

But teenage "time" is strangely fluid, and minutes of feeling centered and connected to Jesus could dissolve into hours of painful isolation. I was lost in the maze of adolescence, and it was my psyche, not my heart, that took control and tried to help me: by slamming me head on into a dead-end.

Chapter 10

With high school life (and life in general), crowded with people and energy that didn't honor the sacred space that allowed the real me to come out, I felt depressed and lacking in control. The summer I turned sixteen I decided I didn't want to eat anymore. I drank coffee all day and ran hard- constantly. My weight spiraled down, and for a moment, I felt in control of something. A bit empowered. It was summer in sunny San Diego, yet I was cold all the time. I shivered and wore sweat pants while others did their best to keep cool and wore short shorts and tank tops. I knew this was changing my body chemistry, but I didn't care.

It was around this time too, that my conversations with Jesus got *heavier*. I got upset at Him for not rescuing me from the physical plane, allowing me to still exist here. Instead of wanting to share the love I felt when connected to God, I wanted to disappear. Life didn't feel good; in fact, it continued to grow sour. I felt stuck between two worlds, utterly confused and lost.

Home wasn't a pleasant place either. I could feel the energy in the air become suffocating among our small family. Such thick tension! I hated being around my dad. His temper got worse, going from 1 to 60 within seconds.

As I contemplated what life was about and my own truth, regarding my faith, I retreated inside myself. I didn't care to connect with anyone because who could understand the depths was inhabiting? Nights were filled with endless journal entries—love letters to God or pages filled with anger. It went back and forth. I wanted to feel special, worthy, and more importantly, loved. I didn't feel loved, and definitely didn't love myself. I was indirectly taught to see myself without worth.

After severely restricting my food and being cold for a good month, I attended my cousin's wedding as one of her junior bridesmaids. At the reception, I was expected to eat, so I did. I was so hungry that it felt good to finish my plate. Horribly, I felt sick afterward; I couldn't help but throw up. At that moment I became bulimic. I figured, great, I could eat and throw up afterward. It was way too perfect: a sense of control and, possibly, a slow suicide.

No one knew this side of me – not my parents, my family, my friends, no one. I think maybe the only people who suspected something wasn't right were: one of the CCD teachers at church who I looked up to, respected, and later became friends with, Mr. Gibson; and one of my teachers from school, Mrs. Fischer. There were a few times when Mrs. Fischer allowed me to sit under her desk and cry. But I never spoke openly to her about my pain or sadness. I'm sure she knew something was up because my grades slipped. I wouldn't have known what to say to her if she had sat me down and asked what was wrong. I didn't know how to answer that question. No one ever asked. Yes, at the same time, I *wanted* someone to ask about me and genuinely be interested in what I had to say. It was as simple as that. There were parts of me that wanted to open up to her, but I thought, what could she do? I couldn't specify in words why I was so unhappy, and at that time, I didn't think there was a solution to this dreadful state. I will always be grateful for her letting me sit and weep under her desk and for quietly respecting my space. It was like an unspoken understanding between us. And till this day, I love her for that.

My other saving grace, Mr. Gibson, met me at Starbucks now and then and talked with me for hours about life and faith. I had met him at confirmation camp. Other kids took advantage of the weekend to hang out outside of school with each other. Me? I walked out of the cabin to talk to Jesus in my mind, asking him why I was there, as religion no longer resonated with me. I spotted Mr. Gibson sitting on a tree stump, looking deep in thought.

"Hey, what are you doing out here? Why aren't you in there with all the other kids?" Mr. Gibson probed.

"I wanted some fresh air and some time with myself. I find it more peaceful and easier to connect to my faith that way. I mean, isn't that why we're here? To go deep into our faith and not so much to become part of a social circle?" I flippantly replied.

"Ha, you've got a point. Perhaps that's why I'm out here as well. Taking all of this in from a deeper perspective and without the distraction of the outer world."

"Yes- the distraction of the outer world. It feels unreal and shallow. How do we permanently escape from it?"

"You don't. You learn to assimilate as you continue along on your own path…"

I felt his energy and intuitively knew there was more that he was processing that day. I sensed he kept a lot to himself, things deep and purposeful. He reminded me of myself. We spent the next thirty minutes or so talking about faith and life. For once, in the presence of dogma and religion, I felt I had met someone who believed in faith the way I did. He was probably the only person I spoke with in depth during that time of my life. There were thirty years between our ages, yet we discussed life, religion, spirituality, and our internal sadness, as if colleagues. I leveled with him, he leveled with me, and I felt important enough to be listened to for once. I will forever be thankful for the way he lit a candle during my life's darkness, through our coffee shop conversations and later by helping me accomplish a big feat in life. He acted like an Earth angel, weaving in and out of my life, trying to save me. But as I believed with Mrs. Fischer, he wasn't capable of that.

What could they really have done to deliver me from my gloom-filled world? I felt too stuck in this place and thought only death could rescue me. I later realized that the only person in this physical life who would save me would be *myself*.

I fought with bulimia on and off for a few more years. It was such a disgusting disease. I can't tell you how often I almost choked on chunks of bread or even noodles when throwing up, too many times to count. My right hand, the hand I stuck down my throat to induce vomiting, had visible dark scars right below my knuckles from my teeth. The enamel on my teeth thinned out. And, unfortunately, my digestive system was badly affected.

My unhealthy addiction continued after high school, and like other people who don't love themselves, I got into an unhealthy relationship. It was filled with so much anger and insecurity. Although I knew I should break it off, I didn't feel as alone as I had for so long, and it offered a constant escape from my house.

A glimmer of hope arrived since it was time to consider the next phase of my life - starting my college career! I wanted to major in psychology to study the mind and human psyche, and to possibly gain an understanding of my own emotions and mental state. I carried more than a full load and worked full time. I wanted to finish fast. I wanted to get away from home.

Unfortunately, the winds of change blew in my direction, and due to something occurring during finals week in my first year of college. I failed every final. This *thing* that happened is not mine to share, and I shall not take that responsibility from another. Till the day I take my final breath, I shall keep this safe within my heart. I cannot in good conscience go into details, but suffice it to say that the shock and sadness of events during that time obliterated my ability to focus and study on my schoolwork, or on anything else, for that matter. (And as time races away, the hands of karma have slowly balanced out any karmic debt this had on anyone. This, like everything else in life, had purpose. I didn't see it then, but I now clearly see the role it played in my life. It was quite the experience that has only helped me evolve throughout the years.)

The incident rocked my faith and shook me terribly. I felt like God had forsaken me. For once, I questioned if there was a God, and if everything magical and spiritual I had ever experienced was real or something I had made up. The hope of a beautiful life and a fulfilling love shattered like glass thrown toward a brick wall. If I had been uninterested in life prior to then, what did I have now to help keep me moving forward? The last thing I wanted to find out was that I was wrong all along and none of it was real.

My dreams mirrored my outer world, becoming more intense. Ironically, I felt increasingly sensitive to the Spirit world. Dead people came into my dreams and told me how they had died and where they were buried. Some would ask me to relay messages to their families or tell their families where they were. I felt shaken up as I awoke from those dreams and avoided thinking they might be real or that I could possibly help someone out there. I was too afraid to do anything about these haunting night visions.

A different facet of spiritual life presented itself: synchronicity. I was introduced to people inclined to explore the spiritual world. I met intuitive individuals who gave me hints of what I would do in this lifetime, who I would be, what I was capable of, and the beautiful life ahead of me. I reminded myself of things I had been told growing up -how my life would unfold. It was not a sure contract with the Universe that this was how my life would eventually be; I knew I had free will and control, but this definitely helped me feel a little bit hopeful.

At about this point in my life, I exchanged my bouts with bulimia for a new, seemingly healthier lifestyle. I spent a lot of time processing my anger and sadness through prayer and meditation, but also through running and consistently going to the gym. And as I became more active than usual, I realized that I needed to feed my body and feed it well. My eating disorders were never about image or physical aesthetics. My battle with them was, in part, to gain some kind of control in my life, along with hopes of a slow suicide. As I finally dropped the addiction and focused on being physically healthier, I knew it would take time to fully heal mind, body, and spirit.

This led to my awareness that the time was right to attempt to end my unhealthy relationship. I decided I no longer wished to lie to my coworkers about where I had gotten my bruises. I wasn't a good liar to begin with, and well, it was obvious they were marks from another's fingers from gripping me so hard. I'd had it with questioning whether a moment would be my last, as he (six-foot-four and over 200 pounds), pinned me down. It was exhausting. We had horrible fights, and I'm sure I didn't make them any sweeter. My anger raged well beyond normal, as did his. Our fights consisted of the two of us yelling, and then me being physically overpowered.

I was conscious of the fact that being with this person was harming me on many levels. I tried to justify his anger and even blamed myself for getting him so riled up. I would think, *Well, I'm just as angry, and I'm just as horrible*. My self-esteem and self-worth dwindled to almost nothing. However, being alone would be even more horrifying – I didn't want to face myself. I was so comfortable in my discomfort, I made excuses that prevented me from doing what was best. I constantly battled internally over whether it was a good idea to end it. Of course I knew I should leave, but I rationalized, to avoid the part when I actually had to follow through with my decision. I was so insecure that I needed to be with someone, even if that person put my physical, mental, emotional, and spiritual health in jeopardy.

The conflicts prevailed. I knew I was enabling this unhealthy connection to continue. I was anxious about what could happen during our fights. Even though I had wanted so badly to end my life before, I was starting to have faith and hope again and didn't want to quit on myself. I wanted a chance to see if I could make happen what those intuitive people ha said could happen. At the same time, I worried that if I completely dropped him, he'd get super angry and come after me. Who knows what would happen then? So I ended it but kept a tiny bit of contact as I weaned him out of my life. I constantly prayed to Jesus and God to protect me and keep me safe from consequences of my decision to ultimately leave this connection for good.

In the meantime, I casually saw someone else, but this was a bad idea. Unfortunately, in the beginning, this new man didn't make me feel worthy either. (I still thought that was a partner's job.) It hurt my self-esteem every time I went to his place and saw his ex-girlfriend's picture displayed on his nightstand. It was obvious he was still in love with her. But being with someone physically, temporarily filled a void. A part of me felt wanted even though I knew I wasn't loved. I'd settle for this in the short-term and work to alleviate that emptiness permanently later on.

I was ten years his junior, and the entire time we were together, I felt like I had to prove myself: that I was mature enough or capable enough or smart enough to be considered good enough. Although our relationship ended shortly, we kept in contact throughout the years, developing a deeper relationship. He fell in love with me, and I loved him too, but not in the way he needed. After failed attempts to secure a friendship, I removed him from my life once and for all, hoping he would find healing and fulfillment with someone else.

(Through writing this memoir, I see how often I desired a loving connection, but was only able to become involved with people who reflected how much I loved myself at the time.

And when I wasn't loved into wholeness – the usual romantic fantasy – I'd still attempt to keep the person in my life, appreciating their contribution to my soul's unfolding story and growth. I've learned, sadly, that's not necessarily the plan.)

As I moved past this relationship, I focused on a new goal. I had initially pursued a career in finance to demonstrate my maturity level, but now I had a new objective, financial independence.

Chapter 11

I never thought I would work at a bank. My employment situation was initially part time. I thought it would be a temporary gig while I shifted direction and reorganized my path. When I first got hired, I wasn't expecting the pressures of making daily, monthly, quarterly, and yearly numbers. My impression was that bank employees just stood behind the counter, looked pretty (they always looked well put together), and processed customer transactions. I never knew it had anything to do with sales. That turned out to be the point of the banking industry: sales and profit. And there I was, a hungry shark in the making. I was trained well and became fairly good at closing a sale.

This was when bank employees were overly rewarded for their numbers. I mean hefty bonuses, fancy meals, extravagant parties, Vegas, all kinds of trips. Plus the drinking, sex, drugs, cheating, and lying… definitely one chaotic and messy environment. Don't get me wrong, I met some awesome and wholesome individuals. I met a few of my lifelong friends working at the bank, like my friend William. We trusted one another, sharing our deepest darkest secrets. Throughout the years, we matured and battled life in tandem, celebrated wins together, and empowered each other to keep rising. I'll always have a special place in my heart for my William-love. Not everyone at the bank was demeaning, scummy or filled with ego; some of us were pretty cool and well-intentioned.

Within my first couple weeks, the branch manager, a banker, and another manager were fired or put on leave due to gaming. Consequently, the branch lost its strong foundation: the leadership of upper management. Previous employees were questioned and interviewed by Johnny, the legal and compliance guy who did investigations. Nobody wanted to see him enter the branch with his black briefcase, because that meant *someone* was in trouble and most likely, going to be fired. Our workplace was in shambles. The result: I received the best training I possibly could. I was thrown in the deep end and allowed to learn hands on. Because the branch was so busy, I had no other choice but to learn a lot of things - and super quickly (even duties outside of my job description). This was a huge benefit to my growth. The more experience I gained, the more I learned, the better prepared I was for additional responsibilities in the future.

After a couple months of running around like chickens with our heads cut off, we were given a full management team and the "cake" branch was back in full effect. For most of us, going through such a crazy ordeal fostered a strong bond. We were more than a team; we were family. However, the pace remained fever-pitch. That branch was called the cake branch in our district for a reason. We had a ton of traffic, which meant zillions of opportunities to make sales, which ultimately meant huge numbers at the end of the day. Everyone wanted to work at this branch, and I was lucky enough to have started there. Because it was so busy, I got really good at sales and learned how to help run a branch correctly. This helped me get promoted after only a few months, and about a year later, I became a service manager (one of two managers in charge of service and compliance).

It was right before the summer of '06, and I had been working at the bank for about a year. I was optimistic about creating a career within the banking world and dedicated my focus to climbing that good ol' ladder of success in corporate America. I no longer cared about going back to school. Instead, I wanted independence, so I worked hard to get it. I was making decent money for a twenty-one-year-old and put a good amount into savings.

Unfortunately, that same year, my parents let our house go into foreclosure. After a few months, the situation remained dire. I remember handing my dad a check to help out for the month, yet a couple weeks later, we were evicted from that apartment. I didn't ask any questions; I didn't dare. My parents were already bombarded with questions from everyone else, and I didn't want to deal with whatever response, or lack thereof, I would be offered. Obviously they were going through significant financial problems. A lot of things happened, and our world grew unrecognizable. There was a huge lack of communication within our family, and we kind of went with the flow, though the flow was abrupt and painful. Although I did my best to help out and took the initiative to look for a home each time we needed to find a new one, *home* was nowhere to be found on any level, whether in the physical realm or at the heart level. It was a heavy time for my family.

An emotional distance widened between my parents, fighting intensified. Dad dealt with his thyroid issue, receiving radiation treatments. To make it worse than it already was, his sister died that same year. I hadn't seen Dad so broken since we parted ways for the first time when I was a little girl. Unfortunately, he wasn't able to fly home for her funeral. And due to the tension between him and my mom, he was left to grieve on his own. My heart ached for him, but I felt helpless and didn't know what would relieve him of his pain and troubles.

I look at my parents as a sad outcome of a once harmonious romance- a beautiful connection that fizzled out due to stresses and pressures of this vain and material world. They chased a dream sold to them, were promised a happily-ever-after, and believed that following the *rules* would bestow on them a sense of completeness and continuous applause from those in their world. Little did they know, happiness is found beyond the superficial and in moments shared with those dear to you. Leading a fulfilling life was about matters of the heart and the spirit, not the stupid materiel crap we yearn for and collect in this surface-level world. I wish they had known this. Maybe deep down they did, but got caught up in a competitive culture.

Dad's anger at life was relentless, and Mom had reached the end of her patience. This new dynamic made being around them extremely uncomfortable. He was infuriated, realizing he no longer had control over my mother (or anything or anyone else really). My mother was fed up with him and his ego and pride. She was cold and not so empathetic herself; she, too, had lost the tenderness she'd had throughout the years. Dad's growing irritation with her lack of understanding fostered in him a deep sadness, his own cave (when he wasn't terrorizing everyone else's.) I knew that the missing piece was simply being able to come together with compassion for one another's worlds, making the effort to understand and empathize with one another. Unfortunately, without proper communication, an open mind to hear each other out, and a willingness to take responsibility as opposed to blaming, they would never fall onto the same page. Ultimately this drove their hearts further apart. I slowly watched my parents disengage from one another. It was like suffering a lingering death, waiting for it to end.

As the family temperature grew intensely cold at home, I went inward and toward that which had always been my saving grace, my faith. I dove into spiritual mysteries, processing weird spiritual dreams or visions I had during meditation, reconciling new revelations with my existing understanding. I felt like I was being given clues again, and sought answers, piecing together childhood hints. Although sometimes frustrating, I felt excited because it gave me a sense of purpose and being.

Perhaps that alerted the Universe that I was ready to make a spiritual leap, for around this time, my friend, David, introduced me to his mom, Mama Jean. I had known of David since middle school but was never introduced until I started working at the bank. He was a banker they had brought in from a different branch to help out when our store was understaffed. After connecting with him on the subject of spirituality and sharing my stories, experiences, and dreams, David thought it would be great for his mom and me to meet. Apparently, she had channeled Spirit a couple times and had a few spiritual experiences similar to mine. He picked me up in the morning before work to drive me over. To be frank, I wasn't sure what to expect. My thoughts were all over the place regarding what could come from this encounter.

The night before, I'd had a dream in which I was returning library books, but as I looked down at the card inside the first page of the book (the one used to sign library books out), I saw a letter on the line where a name should have been. It was the letter C, and I remember a voice whispering, "The name you look for starts with a C." In the car on the way up, I immediately asked David what his mom's name was. To my disappointment, her name didn't start with a C. *Bummer*, I thought, *I guess not all my dreams have meaning. It must have been a random dream.*

Walking through the door, I was mesmerized by how beautiful and grand her house looked.

Without saying hello, a woman (who I assumed was his mother), shot out commands to David, "We'll meet in my room. Bring in a two chairs and two glasses of water." She was gorgeous. Slender and petite in size, fair with smooth skin, and long, beautiful, dark brown hair.

"Hello. It's nice to meet you," I timidly greeted her.

She rushed past to grab white candles from an altar located in the hallway outside her room. I assumed it was an altar, it was filled with spiritual figurines like Jesus and Mary, along with crosses and rosaries.

"I have messages for you. They want to talk to you," she

said, speaking rapidly.

Who wants to talk to me? What's happening? What's so urgent?

She hurried me into the room where two chairs faced one another. White candles and a couple glasses of water sat on a side table. I walked in, noticing how beautiful her bedroom was. Her bed was enormous. Everything was decorated extravagantly, with big plush furniture and floor-to-ceiling curtains that greatly emphasized the height of the ceiling. She motioned me to take a seat as she took the other, leaving David to sit on the floor facing us.

"Sit," she insisted, so I sat. She smiled at me and repeated, "I have messages for you. They're adamant that we do this and that I tell you these things. They're really happy that you're here."

I was still trying to figure out who "they" were, but she quickly closed her eyes and started to pray. She opened her eyes and talked to me with a slightly different tone and altered aura and vibe.

"Child, we are so happy that you're here. We get to finally speak to you this way and let you know of things coming. You know why you're here."

"I actually don't know why I'm here…"

"You've known of Us this entire time. You see, you have a mission and purpose to be fulfilled in this life. You have been searching for a long time, since you were a child. The heavens and that which is beyond this physical plane are rejoicing that you are here being given this confirmation of its existence. You have secretly and quietly known this your whole life. We've been watching you and guiding you. And we know that you look for answers."

"Yes, I look for answers to so many questions- questions nobody else would understand."

"It's in your name. It's in your name, remember that. Also, it's time you accept yourself. Do not be ashamed of who or what you are. Don't be afraid; you're being protected. But the answers you seek are found in your name. You need to remember this. We are watching you and guiding you. The mission you have set for yourself, you cannot and will not fail."

"Please tell me, what is my guardian angel or my guardian's name."

"You have a lot of guardians, a lot that protect you. I cannot tell you their names yet. But we will tell you this: one has a name that starts with the letter C."

As they said this, David's mom smiled—more like smirked- that confirmed my dream. I knew that they knew what I knew, and they knew that I knew that they knew. All was known, and confirmation was set.

She pointed and looked up and smiled as she said, "There is one like you above you, and that is You in entirety."

I wasn't sure what that meant and it would be a crazy riddle to attempt to solve for years to come.

"Furthermore," she said, "you will complete your mission. You will triumph over obstacles along the way. A good life is ahead of you. You are on your way out of the storm. It has started to move past you. Keep going, child. You are protected. You are our star."

As she leaned back whispering that last line, I felt the energy leave, and it was her again in her body. She looked at me with awe. A lot had been said and revealed and confirmed. My only focus would be to keep going, even if my world had felt dark and cold the last fifteen years. My home life was in shambles, and I'd needed some kind of light. And here was God's grace shining on my path, confirming that there was, indeed, more than this sad little world that I found myself in.

And sure enough, being open to new life lessons, I was soon introduced to someone who changed the direction of my life.

Chapter 12

I met Paul.

Paul was a good friend of David's, and I didn't know this, but prior to our dating, Paul would come into the bank to visit David to catch a glimpse of me. He hoped to strike up a short conversation or two with me, in between customers. After months of secretly crushing on me (everyone knew but me), and a handful of attempts from friends and coworkers to bring us together, it finally happened – but not before a false start.

I was invited to Taco Tuesday with our friends. They saved me a seat next to him, but stupid and naïve little me, I pulled out a chair from another table to sit next to one of my girlfriends instead. We left the restaurant that evening without getting a chance to connect and converse.

The next day, the boys at work gave me a hard time about it. I acted like I didn't know what was going on, but I apologized for my aloofness and for making Paul feel rejected anyway. I asked one of the boys for his number so I could touch base with him, thank him for coming out, and suggest we hang out again soon.

That evening, we talked on the phone for a good couple hours, ending the conversation with plans to get together the next evening. And from then on, I probably saw him close to every day for the next eight years of my life.

Paul and I were quickly infatuated with each other. And I fell in love with him fast. I had never felt admired and adored like he made me feel in the beginning. Attracted to him physically, I was also in awe of his musical talents. Ours was a young love that seemed like it had the potential of being a full-blown, grown-up and mature relationship, but unfortunately it didn't live up to that potential. From the get-go, we acted on insecurities, fear, and the need to control. We lusted after one another and confused a passionate love life with actual love. When things were great, they were tremendously great. But when things were bad and shit hit the fan (because shit always hits the fan), they were really bad. It was a crazy roller coaster that distracted me from what I needed to focus on and give attention and love to: myself. I didn't know how to work on myself then, but, probably, I was afraid to.

Most people avoid working on themselves because they're afraid. We're afraid to unveil the hurt and ugly that we've hidden below many layers, that make us who we are on the surface. People don't want to hurt or travel outside their comfort zones, therefore they will dodge any kind of exploring and discovering that puts them in that position, period. Unfortunately, avoiding this work only makes that pain, anger, and fear grow. It's like an infection left untreated; it gets worse in time and sometimes becomes a bigger problem.

After six months of dating, we were sharing a twin bed at his mother's house. My family had been evicted from our rental apartment. They moved in with my aunt and uncle. Unfortunately, space was tight there and left me without a place to go, unless I was comfortable sharing one bedroom with my entire family or sleeping on the couch, which I wasn't. That was a tough time, and my heart broke for my two siblings, stuck in the middle. I wanted to shield them from the pain of a harsh reality. Our lives had changed so much within a few months' time. But although we'd lost our home, our sacred bond endured.

Paul comforted me at this time, reassuring me that although things were rough with my family, I was safe with him. He was there to love and support me emotionally. It was what I needed, and it helped me pull through an ugly patch of life. I remember times where he'd allow me to just cry into his arms as we cuddled in bed. I found solace in him, and loved him for that.

Paul's house was close to work and the best move for me at the time. I planned on staying there until I got a place with a couple friends. It was only supposed to be for a couple weeks, but given my luck, my friends bailed. Actually, it was time to get my own place. I was twenty-one and had never lived on my own. The only problem was the math: I was disappointed with how much it would cost to rent. Fortunately, working at the bank, I came across the mortgage world. After speaking with a couple real estate agents who had partnered with our bankers for mortgage loans, I determined it would be smarter to buy a place rather than waste money on rent. I was young, though, and didn't know where to start. I barely knew what purchasing a home entailed. Undaunted, I quickly made the decision that that was exactly what I was going to do. I didn't know how I'd make it happen, but I was going to!

I stayed with Paul at his mom's place. She was so excited I had made the decision to buy instead of rent and invited me to stay until I purchased a property. I'll always have gratitude for her and the way she allowed me into her home and life.

As expected, that step on my journey was filled with its share of obstacles. I kept crashing into brick walls, but never stopped persevering. I learned at the bank that while we might not always have the answers, we will always have the resources to get the answers and make things possible. That was my guidance system. I pushed onward.

With the help of people around me, after six months of feeling displaced, saving up money, getting assistance from Mr. Gibson, and working diligently towards a pretty big goal, at twenty-one years old, I closed escrow on my first home, a small condo, situated right behind the condo my dad had once purchased for our family.

My family hadn't believed me when I told them I was

buying a home. It almost felt like they didn't want to believe me. Who was I to do such a thing on my own?! I had no help from them and no college degree. From what they thought, I was only someone who worked at the bank. To them, this was beyond impossible and way beyond anything I was capable of. My family always doubted me, maybe not my mom and dad, but my extended family. I repeatedly proved them wrong. My path may have gone against the grain, but nonetheless, I got ahead anyway. I think they hated that about me, like it wasn't fair. I didn't follow the rules, and in fact, did everything quite the opposite. But here I was, doing a lot better than I should have been with what I had initially been given.

I sent my family an invitation to my housewarming party. They came and celebrated with me, but I still felt the questions and doubts. I wanted to scream out loud, "Can't you be a little proud of me for once?"

Having also saved up to furnish my place, I had so much fun picking out everything I needed! For the first time in my life, I understood I could actually make things happen, even if they seemed impossible. I planned to rent out the other room to help pay the mortgage. I was so proud of myself – home ownership and the car of my dreams! I had so much gratitude for life for once. My conversations with Jesus and Spirit were a lot lighter, filled with joy and honor, endlessly thanking them for guiding me to my own home.

In the meantime, I still helped my parents here and there. I strived to rescue my brother and sister during the weekends from an environment filled with sadness, anger, and fear. I wanted to wrap a blanket of peace around them every time I thought of them. I felt for them and did my best to save them, but quickly recognized it wasn't my responsibility, and there was a definite life lesson for them at hand. I knew that, although I could help, I shouldn't try to push or interfere in their lesson. It would grow them, and it surely did later on.

On the relationship front, Paul was finishing school to get

his degree. He moved in with me, and since he was a full-time student, I paid for the mortgage and pretty much everything else. I'll confess that even though I'd accomplished so much, I still felt insecure and desperate for approval and love. Supporting him was how I attempted to get that. I didn't need him to take me out on fancy dinners, give me extravagant gifts or anything of that nature; I just wanted him to love me in return. In the capacity of what I knew of love, I believed that I loved him. I loved his mind and the way he was different from anyone else I knew. He was one of the most talented human beings I had ever met – the kind of musician who could pick up the guitar and play any song.

Apart from our fights, he made me feel (for the first time,) beautiful and truly loved. He always called me by pet names like Babs, cutie, beautiful, or Gracie-baby. Although constantly playing video games, the times he'd pause to be with me, although seldom, felt good. I'd feel safe. However, it was apparent that he had me wrapped around his finger. I would pretty much do anything for him. He knew this. And with that knowledge, he came and went as he pleased. It didn't faze me at all (or so I thought), because I only wanted him to love me back. Our relationship was filled with constant breakups and make-ups after time apart. Many times I'd cry and beg on my hands and knees that he not leave me, throwing away any kind of self-respect or dignity I had left. I was so desperate to be loved. My insecurities controlled any hope to live independently from him. (Talk about no sense of Self!) I always wondered if he enjoyed this control and my need to plead with him not to abandon me, every time we got into an argument.

As much as I did for him, as much as I made it obvious how in love I was with him, I secretly knew he didn't feel the same way. But who wants to believe or admit that? Although he had my heart, I knew I didn't have his. I competed with a ghost who had left his presence long before I came into the picture. He was still in love with *her*. A part of me admired that about him, and a part of me envied her for that. I wanted to replace *her*, but knew that was impossible. She had broken his heart, and my loving deeds didn't move him. Although everything out of his mouth regarding her was negative, I could feel the hurt he held onto and had never healed from and the love he could never let go of. It was a sad story between the two of them. And part of me wanted him to have his happily ever after with this woman he was truly in love with, even if it meant he wasn't with me.

I was in the same predicament as I'd been in with the man I dated before Paul, the one also in love with a previous girlfriend. Here was my chance to finally learn this lesson. To find my own worth and not give in to the jealousy or hurt inherent in this kind of situation. The lesson of learning to love myself stared blankly at me, flashing its ever-so-obvious red flags…but I would not heed the warnings or give it attention for a while longer.

I knew of Paul's ex-girlfriend and had admired her. It was my mistake to compare myself to her time and time again. I fed my insecurities, and he knew where it hurt and would go there during our fights.

"I wanted to do things for her," he'd say, "like surprise her with flowers and dinner and gifts. But I just don't have the same desire to do those things for you. I don't know why."

"I don't get it," I'd reply. "I give you everything you ask for and do so much for you, what am I missing here?"

"You're just not my dream girl. Let's face it, this is all physical, isn't it?"

He knew how to cut me with his words and never failed to do so if given the opportunity.

Our friends had warned me that he was still in love with her, that I was being used and manipulated. I didn't want to believe it. I was so focused on making him love me, that during that process I forgot to honor myself.

I was blindly being conditioned to think that I was not good enough or that I might even be a horrible person. He left time and time again, and even though I hurt and knew I was not to blame for the fight, I constantly apologized, saying it was my fault for everything, and begging him to come home. I learned to hate myself more than I ever had.

Chapter 13

My self-esteem was buried. And, as usual, I turned to my faith and started to read spiritual/self-help books from authors like Dr. Wayne Dyer, Louise Hay, and Jerry and Esther Hicks. I was reminded of the power we hold within ourselves to control our lives, to heal, and to create happiness. Vivid dreams returned.

In one dream in particular, I awakened to a bright, blinding white light. It spoke to me in a voice powerful, yet gentle and filled with love. Right away I knew it was that of Source and of Spirit.

"I want to show you something," it said. A door opened, and it seemed like I was observing different walks of life around the world.

"The world seems pleasant," I said.

"Look again."

As I focused on the scene before me, I noticed ordinary people suddenly turning into demonic figures! Their masks were being taken off, and underneath they weren't as pleasant or beautiful as they had seemed. I watched a man in power lead a large group of people to the basement of a sky scraper as if it were a secret business meeting.

They congregated in a meeting room, and abruptly, the man in power and some other men in power took off their masks and went around, turning everyone else into demonic figures. These horrific creatures swept out to the streets and into the world and started converting everyone else into these hideous beings. People abandoned daily life and purpose and spread hate and fear instead. And the world as I knew it became ugly and lacked love and beauty.

As I cried in fear and disgust, the ball of light closed the door.

It spoke again. "Do not be afraid. You will be among those who will see this play out. You will be able to identify truth — what's real from the false reality constructed."

"I didn't want to see that. It scared me. I don't want anything to do with helping to prevent it, because that means I'll have to deal with the ugly parts."

"You need not be afraid, because you will be protected and guided."

The ball of light handed me a round shield, radiating bright white and gold light. It had carvings on it that looked like ancient writing or hieroglyphics.

"This shield is yours. Do not worry or be afraid, you will be protected. There is much to be done." Before the dream ended, it handed me a white rosary and said, "Here, to confirm the validity of all that has passed between us, take this white rosary and tell your friend Mark Cramer that he should sit in prayer, as he is needing to do so at this moment in time."

I woke up. What a crazy dream. A couple days later at work, my friend and coworker Mark Cramer, returned from his trip to the Vatican.

"Hey Gracie, glad that you're here, I have something for you!" Mark said.

"Hey Mark! Welcome back! How was your trip? Oh wow, thank you for this… white rosary!" *Of course it was a rosary and a white one at that!*

He proceeded to pour his heart out.

"You know, after the trip, I started to feel like maybe I need to pray more. With everything that's going on with my mom's health, and everything else regarding life and career paths. Maybe I need to turn to my faith more and pray."

Remembering the dream, in my mind I quickly concurred. *Yes, Mark, I think that's a good idea. Sit in prayer as much as you need to right now.* I couldn't believe what had just happened. Everything the light told me regarding Mark played out right before my eyes as a confirmation from beyond the veils. My dreams aren't just dreams; they're messages from the other side. That white light and the visions are real. However, I didn't tell him about the dream. I knew it would sound strange, and I didn't want him thinking I was weirder than he probably thought already. I obviously still cared way too much about my image and what others thought of me.

Experiences like this started to happen more frequently. Some sort of light would appear in a dream with a vision or give me the message: "It's in your hands." I had no idea *what* was in my hands or what that meant, but it kept saying that. Getting to meet psychics also picked up. It wasn't like I looked for them. Often, someone wanted to introduce me to someone who turned out to be psychic or intuitive—someone who felt like he or she needed to relay a message to me from beyond this ordinary physical world.

David's mom, Mama Jean, kept in touch and introduced me to a few of these spiritual individuals. One evening, she called me to her house, along with her two sons, David and Dylan. She said that her friend Marie was coming, and she wanted me to meet her. It was so late by the time she arrived, we pushed the reading until early the following morning, and I slept over.

Without my telling her background stories of the mystical experiences I'd had growing up, Marie confirmed intimate and personal information regarding my invisible companion since childhood, Jesus. As she spoke about my connection with Him and the life I had with that particular soul, I sobbed. I knew then that I hadn't made anything up in my mind as a child. My dreams and visions were real. He had been near me that entire time. That was all I needed to know at that point—the simple possibility that I was part of His life somehow, somewhere in a place apart from my current reality. This confirmation filled my heart and being with so much light.

Marie elaborated on a few things regarding my current life as well.

"You know, you worry too much, and you shouldn't. Gracie, you'll always be taken care of. Everything ahead of you is beautiful. You'll always live in comfort and never worry due to lack."

"Yeah, I know I worry a lot. Can you blame me? My life hasn't really been so peachy and happy. It's hard to believe that the remainder of my life will be lived in comfort and in good."

"Well, you know you've got a lot of guides behind you from the other side. You are *definitely* being taken care of...by a whole army!" She chuckled as if that wasn't normal. "I know it doesn't seem like it now, but you won't ever need to worry and money will come easily. You know, you're going to be teaching a lot of people someday about spiritual matters."

"Really, me?! I'm not a teacher, though. I work at the bank."

"Yeah, right now you do. But not for long. You'll see. You're here to teach and heal people."

Apparently, the days of struggle and hurt were passing.

I was so excited to hear this, especially because growing up, my family and I had struggled with money. We weren't homeless or totally poor or anything, but I do remember always being tight on money. I seldom received birthday and Christmas presents from my parents, because, well, I never really wanted anything to begin with, and I understood they couldn't afford to anyway, which was okay. Before I was nine years old, I settled for birthday parties, which were better than presents. My mom invited a lot of people and knew how to throw me a party! I appreciated her greatly for that. Although my siblings got Christmas gifts from my parents, I seldom did. One year, my parents gave them a couple pairs of sweats, but they didn't fit, so they passed them on to me. I was beyond stoked....simply a couple pairs of sweatpants that I *still* wear when it gets cold. This way of life definitely taught me to be grateful for the simple things. I'm not a huge fan of material gifts.

Before we concluded our talk, Marie mentioned one more thing.

"Oh wow...," she exclaimed as she pulled a couple cards out. "Your life will completely be different by the end of the year. Are you and Paul planning on having kids soon? Because you might be with child by the ninth month of this year."

I didn't believe her. I had no plans for that. I had a mortgage and was trying to climb the corporate ladder. I needed to keep my focus. I had worked hard setting myself up for success, and I couldn't let anything get in the way.

Lo and behold, October of that year, I was not feeling well. My coworkers teased that I should take a pregnancy test. There was an ongoing joke that everyone who worked at that branch ended up getting pregnant. When we kidded around about who was next, I never thought it would be me. To my surprise, the test turned out positive. I was pregnant and had mixed emotions. I had forgotten what Marie had told me, until I had a checkup. The doctor confirmed that I was a month along and had gotten pregnant in September, *the ninth month of the year.*

While the timing rattled me, and part of me felt anxious about the changes ahead, another part felt beyond ecstatic. I knew who this soul was. I don't know how I knew, but I felt I had loved this soul before. I also knew it was going to be a boy. I had visions of how he would look—big forehead, cute little nose that would slightly slope up, a ball of a chin, and eyes like mine. I knew him far beyond any words could explain, and I was excited to experience life with him again. Thrilled to be given the honor of being the mother of this powerful and majestic soul, I worried about how Paul would react.

As I anticipated, Paul wasn't as excited as I. His response was that I had caught him off guard. Truthfully, we had *both* been caught off guard. He assured me that he was happy about the news, but unfortunately, I could feel his energy slightly freaking out. This was confirmed by a couple huge fights during the first trimester of my pregnancy. I knew his behavior was due to stressing out over the situation at hand. Things he said and did during those fights were worse than anything ugly he'd done before. Feeling physically ill and freaking out mentally myself, I felt weak - energetically and emotionally, and as he fired off his usual words of attack on my being, I felt beat. His words cut me and robbed me of any self-worth that remained. He threatened to leave. I begged him to stay. He left anyway.

For a few days, feeling physically ill and exhausted as one is with morning sickness, I barely slept or ate due to sadness. I talked to the soul inside of me and reassured him that he was loved nonetheless. Although weak in spirit, I sent love to this precious soul, which in turn gave me back some strength.

Day after day, I waited, as always, for Paul's return. He showed up on Thanksgiving Day. I had been given the task of cooking a dish for my family's dinner party, which I was not looking forward to due to lack of sleep and energy. My mom had driven me to the grocery store to get ingredients. Feeling drained, emotionally and physically, I nearly passed out in the store. My mom had to help me up. I put myself to rest as soon as we got home. *One more... one last try. I will beg him one last time, and after that, I won't ever beg again- I will finally defend my worth and stand my ground, after this last time of begging him to come home.* Which I did—for the sake of Thanksgiving and the growing fetus within me.

He came back, in time for Thanksgiving dinner. Of course, I had to take the blame as usual. I swallowed all of it—my pride, my dignity, and a betrayal to my self-worth—like a huge pill that I knew would poison me in the long run. But I was serious when I pledged that that would be the last time to betray myself. What kind of an example of love would I show this soul if I myself did not learn and practice self-love? I would do us a great disservice in the soul journey we were both on. That wasn't going to be the case. I would unveil truth… which had more to do with Love than I'd ever thought.

Chapter 14

Keoni—that was the name we gave him, the little boy who calls me Momma and with whom I'd fall in love in a way unlike any time before. His name means "God is gracious" and "the righteous one." But to me, his name means "hero," because, well, he's my hero. Keoni is my reason for reawakening into my truth and finally stepping into my own power. I had a rebirth when my son was born. I knew I needed to take control and reconnect with my Self, my worth, wherever I had lost it along the way. This process would take a few years, but nonetheless, the process commenced when the Universe gave me the virtuous task of being this child's mother.

From the onset of my pregnancy, I was aware that the life growing inside of me had a greater purpose than I could wrap my mind around. I felt honored to be the soul that he had chosen to play the role of his mother in this lifetime—to give him guidance to help learn the different aspects of love, how to navigate through this human experience, and to help him grow *tremendously* from it—to become who he truly was. I talked to him daily while he was in my womb, spiritually supporting him with sentences such as:

"Never forget the truth of where you're from. You are Love in its entirety. Always remember how greatly you are loved. You'll never be alone—Spirit and Source are forever with you. Whatever you want to do in this life that honors your highest and greatest good, you will attain. You'll always have help from the other side to complete such feats. Remember that *you* are a mighty creator, able to create instantly whatever right desire you have. And if you act in the name of love, you'll never go wrong."

As the months flew by and my belly grew bigger, I spent most days sitting peacefully in meditation or prayer or reading books. I was so grateful and joyful that my days felt less like a battle against life and more peaceful in every way. I found myself detaching from Paul and slowly finding my own world apart from him. The more I rooted myself in this newfound love experienced in the present moment, the more I took notice of peace and strength growing within my being. I was the most calm I had ever been in my life. Surprisingly, after the last fight Paul and I had, the remainder of the pregnancy was spent in peace with one another.

At about four months into the pregnancy, Paul left for a week, for a cruise for his father's 50th birthday. His mother, his sister's boyfriend, and I, drove him and his sister to Long Beach for the cruise. Before we headed out for the two-hour drive, we stopped for breakfast at a popular new eatery in town. While Paul's mom parked the car, the rest of us went inside to put our names on the waiting list. As we stood in the lobby with a crowd of people waiting to be seated, Paul looked at me and declared, "My ex is here!" In the past, he had jokingly said that. This time he wasn't kidding. She was standing across the way from us with her father.

Continuing with his curiosity and excitement, Paul mumbled, "I think I'm going to go say hi. Yeah, I think I'll go say—"

And he was gone, even before he finished his sentence.

After parking the car, his mom spotted them right away, and she decided to say hello and jump into the conversation as well. After waiting for them to finish, his sister reluctantly also decided to say hi. I stood there with his sister's boyfriend, knowing this was confirmation that I definitely didn't have Paul's heart. I never had, and I never would. And even though I stood across the room from them with his unborn child growing in my belly, I wondered why he hadn't even considered how I would feel if he went to speak to her. I felt invisible and totally abandoned.

My feelings didn't matter. I didn't matter. Had I ever? I'll never know (and frankly, I no longer care). After another few minutes passed, I decided to say hello as well, with my obvious pregnant belly.

As I walked over, I stayed calm. "God, ground me," I prayed. I felt nervousness and heartbreak come into play. I quipped a greeting and started small talk (as if this was normal), while I quietly observed them. He stood at a distance from me, didn't even mention my plain-to-see pregnant state, and never looked away from her. Their eyes were locked, and I obviously had injected myself into their private, little world, clearly interrupting something. I wished I hadn't walked over. I could feel their individual energies reach out to one another. Whether love or simply a wound that hadn't healed, something definitely was present.

My heart broke for myself, for my child, and for *them*. I sort of wished their story hadn't ended. I could tell it had so much depth. I loved this man so much. I wished him the happiness that he deserved, and I knew it wasn't with me. And this painful realization would hurt my son someday. He had never looked at me the way he looked at her, nor had he allowed his energy to ever bow down to me with honor the way he allowed his with hers. I would never fulfill him in the way that he needed. I wasn't capable of giving him happiness, no matter how much I did for him, no matter how much I tried, and no matter how much I wanted to; it wasn't in my power.

If we pay attention and observe our world with a bit of detachment, we could recognize opportunities for clarity and truth. The Universe provides these for us all the time. And not with the intention to hurt us, more so to help us gain insight into where we truly belong. Here was a scenario I had feared, playing out, and if I hadn't been emotionally invested in forcing the creation of a satisfying relationship with Paul, I could have used the information in front of my face to direct my path elsewhere.

Hard to believe, but it would be another four years until I acted upon this knowledge. In the meantime, I wanted to pretend that I didn't know any of that, for the sake of the child that I carried. The week Paul was gone, I cried and cried as much as my little pregnant body could. Then I decided I wasn't going to hurt over this again, after he came back. With that resolve came revelation. I understood why the situation was the way it was, I accepted it, I forgave it, and made peace with it. For the time being, I let it go. I needed to for the sake of my own peace which I deserved.

Rather than remain preoccupied with the outside world, I turned my attention to creating a nursery for Keoni (in the other bedroom that was no longer rented). We painted it baby-blue and filled it with everything a nursery needed: a crib, changing table, new drawers, toys, baby clothes, lots of soft blankets, a never-ending supply of diapers, a chair, lots of stuffed animals, and love. We filled it with love.

I was about five and a half months pregnant when we decided to visit Yosemite with Paul's family. Before the trip, I made an appointment to get my doctor's approval, making sure I would be okay with the elevation. However, we never left the hospital that evening.

"Oh dear..." the nurse exclaimed as she checked my cervix.

"Oh dear what? Is everything okay? We thought this would only take a couple minutes. We're headed to dinner after this. I'm pretty hungry and haven't eaten since lunch."

"I'm sorry, Ms. Divine, but you won't be able to leave for your trip to Yosemite. In fact, you won't be able to leave the hospital this evening or for the remainder of your pregnancy."

"Wait, what? Why can't I leave?"

"Ma'am, have you been in pain at all?"

"No, I've been completely fine. What's going on?!"

"Ma'am, you're dilating and in the process of going into labor, and well, you can't do that quite yet. The baby isn't ready. You've got a few more months to go. So we can't let you leave."

What?! I hadn't felt anything to lead me to believe that any of that was happening. I had been in such a meditative and peaceful state, nothing fazed me, not even physical discomfort or pain. I wasn't surprised I hadn't felt contractions. I was put on bed rest until the baby's due date, which would be another three and a half months. Initially they had wanted me to stay at the hospital for that long, but I begged them to allow me to go home so I could stay in my own bed, in my own space for the remainder of my pregnancy. Finally, on the fifth day of begging, my doctor permitted me to leave the hospital with the promise that I would only get out of bed to go to the bathroom.

So here I was with time on my hands since I wasn't able to work or do pretty much anything else. This was the perfect opportunity to work on myself and prepare for this new chapter in my life. I filled my days with books, writing in journals, and meditating. Dreams around this time were beautiful and filled with peace. Although… I was getting behind on payments and bills because I only received a portion of my salary, my tenant had moved out, and Paul was still a full-time student and didn't work. I stayed calm nonetheless. I had total faith that, although there might be uncomfortable moments coming up, I would nonetheless be taken care of by Spirit.

I didn't want to get on Paul's case for not finding a job. I sort of encouraged him to look for a part time job, but I could tell he had no desire to find one at that moment. In his defense, he attempted to look but never gave it a big push. I understood he was trying to finish up school and wasn't interested in working.

I remembered a pact we had made way before I'd gotten pregnant. I would hold up the umbrella while he finished school; then he'd help hold the umbrella over us afterward. I honored the fact that he wanted to graduate. It was important to him. However, he'd skip classes and play computer games all day. This was nothing new. In the past, I'd gotten so upset because I'd come home late from work, and he'd be on the computer after ditching classes. The clothes in the washer that I'd ask him to transfer to the dryer (so I could fold and put them away when I got home), sat wet in the washer. I'd make dinner, and he wouldn't even sit with me because he was stuck in a "dungeon" and wasn't able to stop or pause the game. Dinner would get cold, and I'd sit there feeling completely unappreciated despite the major efforts I had made for taking care of *us*. I wanted a little bit of his time, his attention, and his appreciation.

That was why we had constantly fought in the past. I knew I didn't ask for much. I wasn't one of those girls who needed to be pampered with fancy meals, trips, gifts, or constant compliments. I enjoyed my alone time, and needed it, in fact. (Now, when recounting those times when I was not loved the way I wanted to be loved, I see how easy it is to blame the other person for their lack of generosity. But I did not belong there, there was more than enough evidence that I would not get what I wanted or needed from Paul. So who is actually responsible?)

Although desperate for connection with Paul, being pregnant, my focus shifted enough to take the edge off my craving for it – and on to giving love to my child and preparing for motherhood.

That was the catalyst for the energy between Paul and me to change. I no longer needed to be needed, to be loved, or to win approval from him. I realized my truth, and started to discover who I truly was, someone who was worthy of happiness and love. Whether exhausted from the unhealthy dynamic of our relationship or not giving a damn anymore, I made up my mind. It was time to work on creating more peace in all areas of my life.

As I quietly worked on myself, magic floated to the surface: dreams with auspicious messages, mystical experiences, and sensitivity to things invisible. I was as still as one could get- the veils thinned out around me, and I finally saw truth for what it was in the physical world.

Open to receiving spiritual teachers and experiences, I happened to be introduced to another intuitive lady, Salma. Of Persian descent, her readings were like those of an old fortune teller, surprisingly filled with a great deal of wisdom. She echoed Marie's message.

I knew I wasn't supposed to leave my bed, but after a month, I escaped to visit Salma for a little bit. As I sat on the chair, I rested my worries and excitedly looked forward to whatever message she'd have for me. Her voice was deep, a little hoarse. I admired her perfectly manicured nails as she flipped the cards on the table. She was beautiful even at her ripe age of 77. She hardly had any wrinkles. Her dyed-brown hair was styled, and you could see she still cared about her appearance.

"The storms in your life are about to pass. I don't know why you're here. You will live a life with so much abundance that you will never have to worry about your well-being. I worry about the people who come to see me. But with you, I don't worry. All I see are endless days of comfort, peace, and happiness. You will do good things in this world, you'll see. People will talk about you. And you will help people, a lot of people. You will do work as I do. You will travel the world and have a husband who will love you tremendously. And the child you carry now, you should know, is very special. He's going to be a holy man. You shall teach him. But go, because you have nothing to worry about. You are well taken care of, child. There is a legion of protectors and holy ones behind you, guiding your every move. You are protected from the other side by invisible holy men. You will live a good life. You shall see. Soon you shall see."

I held on to her words as if they were a life jacket thrown to me as I exhaustingly treaded water. It was a message I'd heard many times before in various ways, but something solidified in me: a deep knowing that there was more to existence than just showing up for life's typical routine. There was this thing called purpose. And if that was so, there was an obligation or duty to follow through. If I did that, I knew I'd be protected and guided by the other side to live out my destiny. I needed to keep doing the work and trust that I'd get there safely. I continued to meditate, grasping a deeper understanding of my truth.

Soon I'd have to make huge leaps into the unknown toward my purpose in life, whatever that might be. It wasn't clear yet. But in the meantime, I focused on the baby developing, because I figured this was part of my purpose as well. As my due date inched its way closer, the idea of giving birth didn't freak me out because I had created peace within my being. Bed rest was meant to be. It created the opportunity to sit in stillness for days and months to reawaken to my truth. The soul I carried was in on it, helping me evolve, and I hadn't even met him in the physical yet.

After a tasty Mother's Day dinner, when we retired for the night, I noticed mild contractions and thought they were probably Braxton Hicks, nothing to worry about. But Paul started timing them and realized they were too close together. They weren't painful, just annoying, so I didn't think much of them. There was no discomfort, only a little bit of pressure. I refused to leave to go to the hospital. But when I sat up in bed to get more comfortable, Paul got the car ready and said we were going to the hospital anyway. When we arrived there, it turned out I was almost 5 cm dilated.

The nurses were amazed I hadn't been moaning or yelling

in pain. I laid there in triage, focusing on my breath as I had in meditation. I recall the screams from the lady next to me. If anything, that was more frightening than the thought of pushing my baby out. They told her she was doing great, that she was almost at 4 cm dilation. I thought it was bizarre that although I hadn't taken any kind of medication or anesthesia, I was in a calm state of mind and hadn't felt pain. The nurses were also astounded at how calm and quiet I was as I continued to focus my mind on something else: breathing and meeting my son.

At last, at 8 cm dilation, they came in to check up on me again.

"Okay girl, you're right at 8 cm dilation without anesthesia or Epidural, and we haven't heard a peep from you yet. If you go past this point, we're not able to give you any kind of meds, so we need to know now whether you want the rest of this labor to be as painless as you've experienced this whole time. Because if you do, we need to give you an epidural now!"

"I mean, sure, I guess I'll have one. I've been quiet and calm this whole time, let's keep this going!"

After the procedure and a little time had passed, the nurse said, "Well, you're fully dilated now. We're going to go ahead and break your water to get this show on the road, okay?!"

"Yeah, sure, whatever you guys think is best."

But once my water was gone, he kept falling on his cord and started to suffocate. Hearing the heartbeat monitor continuously beep a horrifying emergency signal at random times, indicating that he wasn't getting oxygen, was terrifying. *No, I can't lose you now,* I thought.

With the nurse's hand literally inside of me, propping him off the cord, she said, "Sweetheart, I might have to rush you upstairs for an emergency C-section while my hand is still in you to keep your son off his cord."

I prayed to God and my protectors not to let that happen

and to help prop him up so I could naturally push him out. Fortunately, that was the last time he went into distress. I was able to wait for the doctor to help deliver him.

After a short couple hours of pushing, my shy, sweet bundle of joy, made his way into the world. I met Keoni in the physical, and it was the most favorite moment of my existence thus far. I knew I had met him many times before. It was like embracing an old love as I held him in my arms. It was the best kind of love I had ever felt, and I was convinced it would be the best kind of love I'd ever experience. He was so tiny and beautiful. I couldn't believe he was mine and that I was responsible for him; I'd help him thoroughly experience this thing called life. There were so many emotions running through my exhausted little body. But more than anything, I was beyond elated. I loved him so much already, and I knew I had loved him so many times before. *Welcome back, sweet, beautiful soul; it's quite the honor to be your mother.*

Paul was thrilled too. I had observed his quietness (and what may have been nervousness) throughout labor. But he stood next to me the entire time. When Keoni was finally out, Paul's face lit up with happiness and joy. He held that baby so naturally, and I knew that he fell in love with him instantly.

Lots of people came by to visit him at the hospital. This little soul was already loved by many. This made me happy and proud. After a couple of days, we left the hospital. He was unlike most newborn babies. He didn't cry much but smiled a lot instead. Unlike most new parents, we slept through the night almost uninterrupted. He would fall asleep on my chest as I rubbed his back before putting him into his bassinet.

A few days after we took him home, something happened that confirmed my instincts that he, too, would experience a powerful connection to the spirit world.

One night, I placed a sleeping Keoni in his bassinet, next to our bed (on my side). Paul and I were just falling asleep. Right before my eyes closed, a blinding white light crashed into the room, heading towards the bassinet. Immediately my heart raced. I couldn't move or open my eyes all the way. Then I heard and felt a vibration. Its hum grew louder and louder and louder. As much as I wanted to move, I couldn't. But I knew it wasn't bad or evil. It was white light and felt good and powerful. I wanted to see it in its entirety.

"God please help me; let me move so I can see it. Angels please be present, let me move so I can see this light."

As I finished saying that, I was able to open my eyes. It was gone. The vibration stopped. As I quickly sat up, so did Paul.

"Whoa, what was that?" he asked in bewilderment.

"You felt that too, didn't you?"

"Yeah, what was that?"

I was speechless. Whatever it was, was real. We looked over to Keoni, where I had seen the light crash. He was awake, moving around, making noises like the happy baby he was.

Something from out of this world, light beings or even angels from beyond the realms, had visited him. And if that was the case, I knew my hunch was correct. There was, indeed, something extraordinary about my son.

Chapter 15

As my maternity leave ended, I felt like a different person. Yes, I was now a mother, but it was more than that. I had spent time in introspection, ruminating on where I was in life, and quite honestly, it left me feeling more lost. This part of my life is sort of a blur as I searched to find myself. I did, however, meet a couple of lifelong friends. They were the gifts of that time period, mixed in with other new people that I worked with who, unfortunately, weren't the best influence. I wanted to be social and enjoyed going out more than usual, given that I was a homebody. Maybe I was simply escaping the truth that I was lost and unhappy. I avoided doing the work I knew I needed to do. I wasn't partying and getting drunk every night of the week, but I was forming my own social circle apart from the one Paul and I shared. Although I blissfully enjoyed being a mother and loved every second of my time with my son, everything else was a mess. I wanted to change direction and secretly questioned my relationship with Paul.

In the next couple of years, I slowly conjured up a plan to shift gears. I left my managerial position in retail banking, feeling ready to get my feet wet in the corporate world of commercial banking. (This turned out to be the catalyst for falling out of love with the material world once and for all. But more on that later.)

Shortly after I switched jobs, my home was foreclosed on due to falling behind on payments when I was put on bed rest.

Although Paul started working after graduating, it was too late to save my home. I lost what seemed like the foundation I'd worked hard to create. I didn't worry too much about it, though. I thought about what the psychics had told me about my future- that regardless of hardships experienced in the past or present, my life would one day be completely at peace, without worry, and rooted in security. I believed that, and although I was sad that I had given up my home, I needed to continue moving forward.

We moved in with Paul's grandma in Carlsbad, which lengthened my commute to downtown San Diego significantly. Although Paul had finally proposed, the energy between us continued to shift. I was busy learning about myself, exploring my spirituality, studying deeper mysteries of the worlds beyond this one. I had relinquished the need to win over Paul's attention during his every waking moment. He felt the distance. And believe it or not, I felt horrible but needed to do this for *me*. My soul searched for purpose and answers I could only discover within myself. I needed to *honor* myself and find happiness deep within instead of relying on someone else to create it. Although engaged, I felt I still didn't have Paul's heart completely. Therefore, it was time to start loving myself completely. Why die vying for someone's love that might never be given fully?

As I deepened my journey of Self Love, I met other people to help me find answers.

One day, my aunt asked me to go with her to get her cards read by her coworker's intuitive mom. I declined the invite. I didn't care to go, nor did I want a reading for myself. I'd had my fair share of intuitive individuals read my cards, and they'd told me the same thing. I wasn't interested in hearing anything new at the time. However, my aunt was persistent about me coming along.

"Gracie, you have to go with me. My co-worker said that her mom is making a special exception to see me because she doesn't do readings anymore."

"Auntie, what makes you think it will be worthwhile going to see her if she doesn't even do readings anymore?"

"I was told she was really good. She's old, and she knows a lot. Come on, don't you like this kind of stuff? You don't have to get a reading, just go with me so I don't have to go alone. Come on, please, Gracie?"

"Okay, okay, I'll go! But I'm just going to sit there and listen while you get your reading."

When we arrived at the place, I wondered how this lady would read my aunt's cards. Since readers are different, I was curious about her technique and the kind of clairvoyant she was.

We walked in to a small and quaint looking home. Although, lacking square footage, it felt welcoming inside. The energy was light and tranquil. My aunt's coworker, Mila, introduced my aunt to her mom. Her name was Nanay Flor, and she was a lot older than I expected. I slowly walked to the sofa; they carried on a conversation while seating themselves at the dining table.

Nanay Flor stopped, pointed at me, and inquired, "What about her? What is your name, child? I shall read for you, too!"

"My name's Grace. And, no, that's okay. I'm not getting a reading today. I'm just here to keep my aunt company."

"Hmmm...You need to come back and you need to come back here alone. There's a lot I need to tell you. There's a lot that you must know. And I know that you know what I'm talking about. Come back and see me. Come back alone. "

Her daughter looked at me puzzled and whispered to us that there must have been something she saw in me, because it was unlike her to ask people to come back, let alone to want to read for anyone. Her mom had stopped reading a long time ago. Mila was shocked.

After my aunt had her reading done, and right before we

left, Nanay Flor again requested that I come back— soon and alone. In all honesty, I was curious as to why she wanted me to return, and especially to return alone. I went back the next week.

She welcomed me with such joy. Nanay Flor was livelier this time around than she had been the first time I'd met her. She was so happy that I had come back. We sat down, and she took out her cards and surprisingly, handed them to me.

"Okay, good that you're here, now read me."

"I'm sorry, what?! I don't know how to read. I thought *I* was here for a reading that *you'd* give me."

She laughed. "Oh, child, you know how to read; don't deny your abilities. You know you are different. I know that you are different. You are more powerful and evolved in these abilities than I am. I've meditated my whole life. I feel things and I feel people. And I felt you. You are quite a powerful one but still timid about your abilities. *It's time.* That's your message. *It's time.* You need to start doing what you're here to do. You are supposed to help people. I don't have to flip my cards to read you, I know you. Someday soon, people from all over the world will come and seek you out, you'll see. You will help people tremendously, telling them about truth. *They - Spirit, holy ones–* have come to you- in your sleep, in your dreams, and in your waking moments. You know exactly who and what I'm talking about."

As Nanay Flor finished her speech, I took a few moments to allow it to settle somewhere in my mind and in my being. I mean, of course I had been told some of this before, but how was it these people had such a great sense of who I was but I was still figuring me out? I supposed this was the Universe's way of bringing me back to *my* truth. This time, I felt messages I received from her were obvious and direct from Spirit. Denial of this clarity was futile.

She made me give her a reading that day. As I flipped cards, things came to me as if there was some kind of source feeding my mind information. I knew things about her that I couldn't have known. I didn't know her, but in the ten minutes that I flipped her cards, I felt her energy and her being, and I knew a lot. My whole body felt warm, tingly, and I could feel my heart beating fast. I felt sweaty, and in my gut there was movement- a shaking, a trembling of being, I suppose. Spirit was present. I could feel them. And she laughed the entire time as if to confirm that she'd spoken the truth about me. I *did* know how to do this, if I only stilled myself, honed in, and listened. Why had I never listened? Maybe I was too busy talking back to Spirit.

Nanay Flor also did a reading, telling me about my life, what my future entailed and bits of information I was not ready to hear and didn't want to believe were real. I refused to accept them as part of my destiny and a part of me. (In later years, no matter how hard I fought against them, I wound up feeling exactly how she said I'd feel and experienced each of the events she had mentioned.)

"Never forget me," Nanay Flor said. "Keep me in your my meditations. I meditate every day, and I'll do the same for you."

Not long after, Nanay Flor moved to northern California, and I never saw her again. Until this day, I keep her in my thoughts.

After our meeting, I made the conscious decision to move in the direction of manifesting the prophesies I'd been told. What resulted was heightened sensitivity: I saw colors, auras, and energy. I was feeling things and had deep insights about new people I met. I kept quiet about it, but internally, it felt like I was going crazy.

I looked up programs and classes about the metaphysical world and my experiences, and discovered a place that offered classes in Hillcrest, San Diego. It called out to me, and I wanted to check it out. Fortunately, they were having a "psychic fair" that following weekend, and as busy as my weekends usually were (family events and whatnot), this particular weekend was open. I thought it was a surefire sign that I needed to attend.

I had never explored that side of town. (Little did I know, that's where I'd have an office.) I asked my younger sister to come along in case I got lost or something, and it was a good thing I did. We circled the busy street that the fair was on, and for the life of me, I couldn't find it. It was raining, and there were so many cars and people. Before giving up, I figured maybe looking for it on foot was a better idea. I searched for parking but wasn't successful. As we circled again, still having no luck in locating it, I called out to the Universe: "If I don't find parking, I'm leaving. I guess it's not meant to be…" As soon as I finished proclaiming that, a car abruptly backed up from a parking space right in front of my car, almost hitting us. *Well, okay then. I'll park and we'll go from there.*

Literally, right in front of my parking space, stood a board that read, "Psychic Fair upstairs on the second level," with an arrow pointing toward the staircase. Quite the confirmation and a straight-up wink from the Universe that this was, indeed, meant to be. Upstairs, we explored the different services and information, from aura photography to healing stones to readings and more.

I was pretty amazed at the cool things they offered. I liked the vibe; the people were super nice. Not long after arriving, we bumped into the lady who ran the place; I recognized her from the website. I informed her of my intention to learn more about this.

She looked at me, paused, and smirked. "Actually, it won't be long until you end up teaching this stuff. You know you're here to teach, right? You know a lot more than you think. You're not here to learn; you're here to do something else, like teach the world about truth. You're a Master Teacher."

All I could think was, *a Master what?!* The same messages kept coming my way. And I believed the individuals who were the messengers; there was a different energy in their beings. It felt like the Universe and Source were speaking through them.

"Well, you're welcome to look around," she said.

A woman walked up to us.

"This is Janice. You should have a reading with her."

"It's a 15-minute reading for $20, cash only," Janice confirmed.

I stammered, "Oh bummer, I don't ever carry cash. I'll have to pass..." And of course, as I said that, I unconsciously put my hand in my jacket pocket and felt a folded piece of paper. To my surprise, when I pulled it out, it was a $20 bill—again, confirmation that I needed to be there to hear whatever it was she was going to tell me.

We sat down in a different room. She set the timer on her phone for 15 minutes and asked me if I had any questions. I told her that I was on a journey seeking truth and trying to figure out what I was here to do. But most importantly, for some reason, at that moment my mind took me to the subject of Jesus. I asked her about the connection I had with this soul— this majestic teacher of mine. Why had it always felt so strong? And why had I felt Him since childhood, even before I was introduced to Him at church? Apart from who He was and who the Bible had made Him to be, who was He to *me*?

She started to tear up. "I'm so sorry. I don't mean to cry, but the energy is so powerful and pretty significant. There is definitely a connection. And as I am seeing through my mind's eye, Jesus is kneeling to you in gratitude. I have never seen this or anything like it. I feel that you were definitely a part of his life. You did something for him—something he is tremendously grateful for. You will have to explore and rediscover what it was, in this lifetime. It's part of who you are and a part of your purpose. I know someone doing work on Yeshua and Mary Magdalene. Maybe you should get in contact with her. Her name is Joan. There's a lot that you'll end up doing in this lifetime. There's something you'll be bringing into this world- truth or a message. There's a lot ahead of you, but they want you to know you're greatly guided and protected. You just need to keep going. Even in the darkest of moments, you need to believe and have faith that there are forces beyond this physical world helping you carry out this purpose of yours."

As she wiped away her tears, we noticed that her alarm hadn't gone off. She had clearly gone over the 15 minutes for my reading. She laughed and said that whatever was needed to be said was said. Everything was divinely guided, and so it was...

For the next handful of months, I sought out help and information and explored the spiritual and metaphysical world in depth, taking classes and learning from people knowledgeable in this arena. I read books on metaphysics and about the world beyond the veils, such as The Seat of the Soul, and others written by Gary Zukav, more by Dr. Wayne Dyer, Jerry and Esther Hicks, Paramahansa Yogananda, and Swami Muktananda. I watched a plethora of documentaries regarding various religious and spiritual philosophies, attended circles and psychic events and learned about divination. I learned different meditation practices, attended the Self-Realization Fellowship Sunday services, stopped eating meat for a while, started to practice Yoga, and socialized with people interested in the same things.

Synchronicities happened on a daily basis. I felt like I was being divinely guided wherever I went. I was pretty much following the breadcrumbs placed on my path by the Universe. When they spoke, I listened. When they gave me signs, I paid attention. When the Universe winked at me, I knew for sure this was meant to be. It was more than what was happening on the surface level; it was everything affecting me internally. I was changing, opening up. I even bravely explored dark areas of my soul that hurt and were hidden from the outside world and from my own conscious self. I confronted these parts of myself and started to heal them by shining light onto them. I looked at my life, at what I was still angry with, what I was holding on to, what I hadn't forgiven, what and whom I resented, why I was not at peace with certain things, and why I was not at peace with mySelf.

I investigated these issues. And I asked myself whether I was honoring myself by doing certain things and being around particular people. Was I in a place leading me to my highest and greatest good? The answer was…no. I wasn't quite ready or brave enough to change. But I did continue to examine who I was: the ugly and the beautiful, and I gave love to the duality as best I could. Learning about the Self is crucial to developing the ability to love thyself. You cannot learn to love yourself if you're unwilling to know yourself.

I ended up calling Joan, the lady whom the psychic had suggested I contact. Going off on a tangent regarding what I called her about, we talked about channeling in great depth. With Joan's help and instructions, I started to do that. She said that Spirit would assign me a guide, and before we started, she warned me not to get disappointed if the guide chosen or whomever wanted to step forward was not some great saint, master, prophet, or guru. As she turned her cards over, though, she started to chuckle.

She chuckled. "Your guide, whom you'll be channeling, is Siddhartha Gautama."

Puzzled, I asked, "Sid who?!"

"Siddhartha Gautama, you know, Buddha?!"

"Ohhhh, the fat dude."

She laughed even more. "No, not that one. Siddhartha Gautama, the ultimate Buddha, the first Buddha. Look him up."

"Okay sure, I'll look him up one of these days…"

I was disappointed that she had not said Jesus or some

other saint popular in the books that I knew of. Unfortunately, I didn't know much about Siddhartha Gautama. In fact, I thought he was the fat Buddha, when ironically, he was the very thin one who had fasted and meditated up to his ascension.

I started to do "automatic writing" while channeling not just Siddhartha Gautama but other spirit guides of mine as well. I was astonished by what I was writing: messages from Spirit, information regarding spiritual truths of initiations, the pyramids, and other mysteries I hadn't known about. I explored the things I wrote about while channeling Spirit. There were numerous ancient mysteries, many I didn't initially feel comfortable with, considering my religious background and what I'd believed in before.

One day I brought up the original reason I was supposed to contact Joan.

"Hey Joan, I heard you were doing work on Yeshua and Mary Magdalene. I'm interested and wondered what your research was about," I said.

"Well, it entails uncovering the true details of Jesus' life after He was crucified. There's a lot that's actually written about it, but it's not talked about."

"Hmm...rrrright," I reluctantly agreed.

"I wrote a channeled book about it, maybe you should go read it. In fact, I'm being told by Spirit that you should definitely take the time to read it."

"Ummm, yeah okay. I will, one of these days..."

"Seriously, you need to read the books of John in the Bible."

I rejected the idea. I had put away the Bible years ago and felt it no longer benefited me in my spiritual exploration. (Later I discovered how wrong I was.)

While I learned from Joan about the spiritual world (how to properly communicate with Spirit and how to control certain abilities), I also took classes at a temple in Encinitas to further develop these skills.

The idea of past lives kept being brought up. Coincidentally, I was seeing a spiritual counselor who brought up past lives and asked if I was open to being regressed. Out of mere curiosity, I gladly agreed.

Shocking, familiar... my experience the following week blew me away.

Chapter 16

The first thing I saw were my feet, wearing sandals. I examined my body to specify whether I was male or female. Definitely male. I immediately knew it was biblical times based on the people and environment. I heard a few voices call out to me, turned around, and realized I was walking with a group of men. I was lagging behind, and they wanted me to hurry up. One of them told the rest to continue along, and he walked down to me. And as I looked at who approached, right then and there, I felt warm and tingly in my body, and I started to cry. I knew that face, beautiful and familiar...Jesus. I felt like I was home.

He smiled at me and said, "Well, John, what is it that delays you?"

As He walked closer, I was filled with a sudden and overwhelming emotion of fear and sadness. Almost paralyzed in a state of apprehension. My present self was a bit confused as to what was happening and where those emotions were coming from, and surprised at how real they felt.

"I'm scared. I'm not sure I can go through this."

"Do not be afraid, John, you know what to do." He spoke very quietly. "We have talked about this. Everything will be taken care of. I need you to be brave. Everything is set. We need to follow through with plans at hand. You'll see, everything will fall into place. You know what to do. Don't be afraid."

What was it that I knew to do? My present self was more confused than ever. What was I afraid of? And why was he whispering? Why didn't the others know of the secret plan at hand, or did they?

The next scene was that of Jesus being crucified on the cross. At this glimpse of such a horrible scene that always filled me with tremendous grief, I sobbed and could not help but feel tremendous fear and a sharp pain in my gut. My friend was dying on a cross. I stood beside His mother and Mary Magdalene, who also wept, in pain from this ghastly moment. Guards walked around, and as they walked away for a moment, Jesus caught my attention and quietly whispered, "John, you know what to do. You know the plans to undertake. So much is at stake. Be brave, my brother. Do not be afraid. Carry on with what we have talked about in secret."

Confused and lost, my present self was curious as to what was happening and what was about to take place.

In a moment's time, it was the next scene: before dawn, the world still slept, and I was walking through what seemed like fog. In the semi-darkness, I headed towards the shore with a couple others: a man, a woman, and what felt to be the energy of a child. When we arrived, there was a small boat that awaited us. These individuals got into the boat, and I was filled again with complete sadness as I looked up to see their faces. It was Jesus accompanied by Mary Magdalene with child. As Jesus thanked me, I could not help but cry, because although He was not dead on a cross or in a tomb, He was leaving, leaving me for good. In this lifetime He had become one with God, raised His body into this Christ light and fully ascended. I would never see Him in the physical again in that lifetime or any other. In the distance, there was a great ship they would board to take them to the south of France.

Part of me resisted this story, because growing up Catholic, I believed in the story of His crucifixion written in the Bible. This story was beyond that story.

As the next scene arrived, I found myself as an old man secluded from the world. It seemed I had written a lot about truth in that lifetime. And as I lay on my death bed, I uttered the words, "It is done. Thy will be done. All that is truth, I have written in the books." As I finished, I took one last breath as if I had chosen that exact moment to release my spirit back to Source.

That was the end of that life. But there was more. I saw myself rise above the world, and I saw Jesus, along with Mary, welcome me beyond the veils. With His big, beautiful smile, I felt peace and an overwhelming surge of unconditional love. He laughed. "It took you long enough!" And it had; I had spent the last long years of my life writing and sharing truth with those who had ears that intently listened and hearts that were open to the Word. He looked at me again with His piercing stare as if looking into my soul. "My dear beloved, always do in the name of God, of Love. Go and love the world one heart at a time." That marked the end of that past life regression.

Whether these things were true, real, or completely made up from fantasies of a magical world beyond the present, there were too many unknown details for me to have created it. A fire was lit inside of me at that moment which drove me to further explore this mystery. I had so many questions—such as, why the South of France? All my life I had been enthralled with France. Had I injected my own fondness for the country into the regression? In fact, while everyone I knew took Spanish in high school, I wanted to learn French. I had this dream that someday I'd own a farmhouse in the South of France. Why there? I'm not sure; I always felt attracted to that specific area. I knew it was time to push beyond the limitations that I had created, growing up with a dogmatic religious background. However, as curious and driven as I was, I temporarily abandoned the part of my investigation related to France, Jesus, and Mary Magdalene and didn't return to it for another year.

Like other spiritual dreams I had growing up, in another

one, I found myself in my grandma's old house. (Every time a dream was set in that location, I knew it was special and there was more meaning to it than what I would experience in the dream itself.) I was roaming around the house, through the living room, hallways, and bedrooms. It looked like a party or get-together was happening. As I walked past people, I almost felt invisible.

I heard a voice that introduced itself as one of the spirits that was stuck there. It kept taunting me. "Alright, kid, now that you're aware of your abilities, get rid of me. Free me from this place. I challenge you. How powerful do you think you are? Free me... get rid of me."

And with the will to grant it its freedom, I chased it around the house, trying my best. All it did was laugh at me. I returned to the foyer, frustrated and ready to give up. The door was wide open, and I started to walk out, reluctantly accepting defeat.

However, before I reached the door, I heard a voice: "Don't go. You know how to do this. You know how to *bless*. Don't give up now. Use the abilities you have: it's in your hands. Remember, child, remember your truth. Now come back in and bless the house."

The voice sounded so familiar, I couldn't pinpoint whom it belonged to. I turned around to see the same ball of light that had spoken to me in previous dreams.

I told the light, "I can't do this. I'm not powerful enough. I'm not powerful, period. I just don't know how to do this."

"Yes you do. Trust in yourself, you know how to bless. Don't ever forget where you came from and who you are. You know how to *bless; it's in your hands*."

As it repeated over and over that I, indeed, knew how to bless, I awoke to my alarm. I had overslept. I rushed to the train station that morning as I often did, got out of my car, and ran to the train whose doors were starting to close. One of the conductors knew me and always smiled when I jumped onto the moving train, heels and all. That morning, the train was abnormally crowded, and to my surprise, I didn't recognize any of the usual passengers as I aimlessly looked for a seat. Typically there was ample space, this morning was different.

The only available spot was next to a man whom I had never conversed with, due to his nose being in a book every morning and evening. However, when he spoke, it seemed like people respected him. He wore black slacks and a button-down shirt underneath a thick, black jacket to help him brave the morning chill. He seemed like the wise man in the group whom people looked up to, always having something wise and deep to say. You'd think I would have made friends with this fellow by now. In fact, I was a bit intimidated by him in the way a student would be intimidated by a guru or master.

Well, perfect timing. I haven't met him yet. If only he'd take his nose out of his book, then perhaps we could have some sort of introduction. As I sat down, I took my own book out (*Jesus and the Lost Goddess*) and dived into it. I could feel him look up and turn his attention towards my book and then at me.

"I know you. I know who you are. You know how to bless...," he said.

Shocked and feeling almost frozen hearing those words, I turned to him with a sort of gaze that must have requested him to repeat what he had said.

Smiling at me and chuckling at my puzzled reaction, he said, "You know how to bless."

"How do you know that?"

"I know you. And I know that you are more powerful than you realize you are. You know how to bless. You know truth deep inside of you. And perhaps I'm here reminding you of what you know."

"But how do you know me, and how do you know all this?"

"You have sought out truth your whole life, haven't you?

You've disciplined yourself to secretly work on your inner depths. You know very well that there is far more than the reality that you see with your physical eyes. That there is more beyond this physical life and world. You explore ancient mysteries hoping for answers and truth to be revealed. You have felt what truth is. You know the answers and where they are hidden. *We* have watched you and guided you from the beginning of this lifetime. You have been given messages throughout the years, and we've come to you in your dreams and in the physical, hoping you'd finally remember that truth which you seek.

"You see, there's a group of us who have evolved past this physical world—who have ascended and become One. We have promised to aid humanity in its ascension. And to those who awaken and are ready, we approach and give guidance. That is why I'm here, to tell you that you have been one of those individuals. You know the truth, because it's embedded within you and you are starting to remember. Your focus and your efforts to stay on this path have been consistent. I am one of those that watch over you, guiding you along on your journey. Others who aren't yet ready to hear the truth won't believe you. But you will do the work anyway, and you will share with the world that which you know."

"So you're here to watch and protect me?"

"To make sure you do not fail. To help you continue to ascend, to be One with God and to help others do the same."

I realized then the significance of my failure to see a single familiar co-passenger. It was as if time and space had opened up and given me this moment so this man could relay this message.

He told me he would not acknowledge this conversation after today. Then he went on about spiritual laws and secrets of the worlds beyond such as, the misinterpretation of certain religious beliefs and what Ascended Beings do as a group to provide aid to mankind on the Earth and beyond the dimensions. I couldn't believe the amount of wisdom he shared in the short hour-long train ride. As his stop approached, he bid farewell.

"Remember who you are. The answers are within. Do the work, there's plenty ahead. Keep going. You'll know what to do next. We'll always show you which way to go. But for now, go within and do the work."

I couldn't focus on anything else that day. As I looked blankly at numbers and Excel worksheets filled with data on my computer screen, I couldn't help but revert back to my dream and my unusual encounter on the train. *Was he for real? Was he even real?*

Those from different planes or dimensions, more advanced and evolved than we, are able to watch and guide us as we go through the human experience, learning lessons and moving through our own ascension journey. Although usually invisible to the human eye, they are present. At times, they come into the physical and appear to certain individuals or relay messages through other individuals. Similar to how we are guided by angels, we, too, are guided by a group of individuals who have promised to help in the ascension of every soul - The Ascended Masters. I wouldn't learn about them until a year and a half after the train incident.

That evening on the train ride back, I was left in solitude. Again, no one familiar was on board, which left me to sit by myself, watching the ocean as we rode parallel to it. On the way to dinner that evening, I couldn't wait to share my experience with Paul, but he spoke up before I could.

"So...you were having one of those dreams last night?"

"Yeah, I was actually. Wait, how do you know?"

"You were talking in your sleep again."

"I was?"

"Actually, I freaked out, because when I turned over to wake you, I saw a light in the shape of a ball hovering over you, like above you, and it looked like you were talking to it. And then I rubbed my eyes and looked again, and it was gone, and you had stopped talking. But it totally freaked me out at first. So I figured maybe I was still half asleep or something."

"That's exactly what was in my dream! I dreamt I was talking to this ball of light that told me I could bless, whatever that means. But this morning on the train, I had a crazy experience with this guy who told me the same thing…"

As I went on about it, I was pretty sure Paul had tuned me out. I don't think he ever believed me, even when he, himself, saw or felt the extraordinary moments when Spirit decided to come in and validate itself. I stopped sharing, and my mind trailed back to the time a few months earlier when I found out how Paul really felt about my spiritual journey.

Chapter 17

One evening, Paul was hanging out with my cousin's then boyfriend (now husband), and I had just gotten off the phone to ask him about when he'd come home that night. I remembered one last thing to ask him, so I called back. Unknowingly, he answered my call, and I was able to hear his conversation with his friends for a good 10-15 minutes. He pretty much talked about how he thought I was crazy and that it was stupid and almost funny that I believed in what I believed in—that I actually believed I had certain abilities. He thought that the weird encounters I had with psychics and spiritual beings were phony, and that I was going down the rabbit hole, beyond crazy.

This broke my heart once again. And if I hadn't yet been convinced that he didn't love me, hearing that strengthened my assumptions. However, I still wouldn't do a thing about it. I played on and continued with the flow, not willing to take responsibility nor the initiative to stand my ground for that which truly honored me. I think I felt marrying Paul was the right thing. We had a child together, were part of each other's families, and we'd been together long enough that it seemed like the next thing to do. But given my true knowing (even if ignored) of our surface connection, my whole heart was not fully aligning with the idea. There was an obvious resistance from my being that I kept fighting.

As the months went by, we busily planned a wedding. Paul and I quickly realized how expensive it would be to have a wedding in San Diego. We decided mid-year to have a destination wedding instead. (You know how that turned out.) We both wanted to get married near the ocean, and thought this was perfect because we'd say our vows on one of the most beautiful beaches of Cabo San Lucas. We were excited to create our wedding exactly as we'd envisioned: the style (beach wedding), the colors (turquoise and coral), the people (our family and closest friends), an intimate feel, and of course, the cool adventure we would have on the way there. I remember days of really wanting to be married to him, finally being able to be his wife. I'd tear up listening to songs that our friend wanted to play on the guitar and sing while I walked down the aisle. During those days, it felt good knowing I was marrying him. I didn't struggle with the idea that I wasn't completely honoring my heart.

Another major to-do item: house hunting. Since I had foreclosed on my place, we were buying another home under Paul's name. As soon as he started working, he began saving up his money. We searched for property in the San Diego area, and found the cute little community, San Elijo Hills. I emailed our realtor a few of the homes I wanted to check out. One in particular had caught my eye. Unfortunately, every time we wanted to see it, the owner wasn't there or we couldn't get in contact with the other real estate agent. It wasn't meant to be, I suppose. Before the year ended, we found a home located in the town we grew up in.

("Coincidentally," the home I had been drawn to was owned by a man I'd meet a year later. Everything happens in divine timing, and I guess I wasn't supposed to meet my friend Brian yet. But his home had called out to me, and I felt familiar energy. We are always attracted to that. Whether someone is known or a stranger, we'll experience an automatic connection that feels like we've encountered one another before this present lifetime– a bond that cannot be severed. In fact, there is usually a lesson or two or more, entwined in the relationship.)

Many changes were on the horizon, and it seemed everything was falling into place. I had completely quit the financial industry, ready to focus my energy into a spiritual healing practice. I had gotten my Reiki Master Certifications and was working on clients. I had also decided to get my hypnotherapy certifications. I chose hypnotherapy because clients and I were fascinated with past lives, and hypnotherapy would allow me to dive into that field and learn to perform past life regressions. It felt like part of my path.

My own past life regression lingered in the back of my mind. Additionally, I was influenced by a woman at the bank, Ms. Amedee. She was French and probably one of the sweetest and most soft-spoken individuals I've had the pleasure of knowing. A kindred soul, we'd discuss spiritual concepts, our mystical experiences, her trips to India, and studies with her guru. She had the most beautiful, piercing blue eyes I had ever seen. An aware, intuitive, Ms. Amedee validated that going toward hypnotherapy for the purpose of learning more about past lives was a good decision.

When we spoke of lives before this present one, Ms. Amedee constantly told me this lifetime would be my last. She shared a dream in which the Goddess Shiva appeared and showed her that I was with *the* Divine, that I had become One. From my understanding of ascension then, I thought that was impossible. I had way too much karma to clear out, too much work before me to even get close to thinking I would ascend beyond the confines of this physical world, in this lifetime. Nonetheless, she reminded me time and time again that I was more than I thought I was, and this lifetime would be my last. Even after leaving the bank, we kept in touch. Whenever we met up at a coffee shop nearby, we'd converse for hours. She introduced me to her future husband, Luca, after he'd had a vision of me in a meditation and wanted to meet me. The two were the perfect balance of masculine and feminine, though individually they possessed a perfect balance of both energies, too. It would be several years until I believed of me, what they had believed of me.

About to start hypnotherapy certifications, I got an email from Joan (we'd become friends). She said that she had students who had recently learned to read the tarot and was hoping to have volunteers whom the students could read for. Immediately, not even thinking twice, I volunteered, and she paired me up with Victoria. I'm not sure if Joan had intuitively felt that Victoria and I would be a perfect match, considering our similarities, but I was very grateful to be her volunteer. Following the reading, we shared our stories and clicked – an instant friend!

A few weeks after our first couple of interactions, we went to a psychic fair and realized we knew someone in common. The instructor at the hypnotherapy institute I was about to attend had once been her hypnotherapist! In three days' time, she made the decision to travel the identical path as I and enrolled in the same hypnotherapy certifications.

We started class together a week later. I thought, how synchronistic, the manner in which we'd been introduced and the way we had similar journeys moving forward. Victoria became one of my good friends and a close confidante.

I finally decided to read my friend Joan's book. It was about Jesus' disciple, John, and his account of his experience with Jesus, all the way up to Jesus' crucifixion. The book put me on the edge of my seat as I read from beginning to end, nonstop. I felt like I had known these details beforehand. I was familiar with them, and they, in turn, moved energy inside of me. My emotions rose to the surface and I cried the entire time until I finished it. In the end, it read in synchronistic fashion, connecting with my past life regression. It confirmed that Jesus had survived the crucifixion and that he and Mary Magdalene, with child, had sailed off on a ship. Although in the book it did not say where they sailed off to, I knew they were headed toward the South of France. After that, the region's allure grew stronger. I made a promise to myself that I would travel there, believing that I would find a salient bit of truth which would complete me or set me free.

As we moved into the new year, it was apparent that an unknown chapter was about to unfold. After all: new marriage, new home, new job. The energies had changed, and I felt my inner self preparing for a mighty lesson up ahead. It was as if I kept hearing Spirit whisper, "Brace yourself."

Chapter 18

Depth. Purpose. Meaning. Life. Love. Nope.

Why is it so difficult to believe in our perceptions of truth—even with experiential "proof"? You'd think that after one of the most thrilling adventures of my life—getting to my wedding—that I'd accept and understand the power of my connection to spirit. Yet, others' doubts and inability to believe in something grander than present reality slowly ate away at my own faith. I knew I hadn't made up overcoming those hoops and hurtles. There were witnesses! And at the least, I'd shown up! How could they not believe my story?

No one believed in my magic. The new groom included. Although he lit up out of surprise and happiness, I sensed he didn't believe I'd been on a mystical adventure. He believed in my determination to get things done, but beyond that, there was no such thing as magic to him. So when I sat on the ship, I questioned whether the passport fiasco had been Spirit intervening to keep me from marrying him. Had my energy also subconsciously created those obstacles to help me see the signs and red flags? Or had it been me with Spirit co-creating a story that would validate my intuition and connection to Spirit, that I could return to years after the incident as a reminder of who I was and what I was capable of accomplishing? Perhaps it was all of that.

No matter, within a short time, I wondered if I had chased after a marital ghost, arrived at the last room in the house, and it was nowhere to be found. I was left feeling empty. I loved Paul, more than he knew, but why wasn't being married to him enough? Our relationship was not as alive as I'd hoped it would be. I felt like I wasn't good enough around him and that the authentic person I was becoming, was not someone whom he was completely stoked about or who fulfilled him in return. The things I believed in, my faith, magic, love, and a life serving the world - he saw that as ridiculous, un-achievable, and as real as the boogie monster under the bed. In fact, it was hard to forget hearing him on the phone poking fun at my beliefs and laughing at me. However, at times he seemed to play along if it suited him. But he was my husband now, and I depended on him to support my departure from the corporate world for the pursuit of my dreams and passions. Unfortunately, although he did his best, it wasn't enough.

After we got back from our wedding, we decided to try for another child. We thought that perhaps that would resuscitate our marriage and connection. Looking back, that kind of thinking was definitely a huge sign not to go further down that path. You should never try to dig yourself a deeper hole when you think you're in a hole already. Our intentions were misguided, though understandable: having Keoni had been the happiest experience of our life together. We wanted to share that experience with one another again. But for the most part, I think we were hoping for a saving grace. After a few months, without results, we stopped trying. The distance between us grew.

In meditation one morning, I was reminded of what Jesus had told me in the past life regression. He had said, "Go and love the world, one heart at a time." It dawned on me that the other part of that was "starting with yours first."

Aha! Why could I never fill that mysterious void within? What was missing? My love for myself. Before, I had wanted to help the world, but hadn't known that the key was helping yourself, learning about yourself, and loving yourself *first*. How was I to love the world if I didn't know how to love myself? I felt compelled to heal deep wounds of childhood, adolescence, and even from a handful of years back. Learning about my own Self through different stories that have made up my life and the different adventures that have grown my soul, I slowly uncovered the mysteries and questions about life that haunted me as I grew up.

It was challenging to confront those painful moments, and it hurt to realize how I had allowed those moments to negatively impact me and my relationships with myself and others. I was learning to become accountable. Blaming others and the Universe for the hurt in my life kept me a victim. I definitely didn't want to be that anymore. As I started to take responsibility for my life, I knew I would start to gain control of it as well.

Meanwhile, my son was growing up fast. I cherished the moments in the evening when he'd peacefully drift off to sleep as I held his little body in my arms. Oh how I loved those times! We would lie in bed singing classic songs like, "You Are My Sunshine" and "Glory of Love." I told him about angels, that his superpower was Love, and that he was capable of doing pretty much anything as long as he did it in the name of Love. I introduced him to meditation. I'd meditate in my and Paul's walk-in closet, and sometimes I'd sit there for almost a couple hours. Opening my eyes, I'd find Keoni sitting in front of me trying to mimic me. He was definitely *mine*.

Over time, his sensitivity to energy and sounds became obvious. He hated loud noises; they would often distract, scare, or annoy him. He would point to an empty room, corner, or wall, and ask who the people were that stood there. He started telling me that they wouldn't stop looking or staring at him, and he'd compare them to real people, telling me that the man he saw in the corner looked like Uncle so and so. He'd have dreams of people around him from different times and places and tell us how they'd died. And he, too, was independent. Just like me and his father, he knew how to be alone and enjoyed it.

I'd like to think that the connection we have as mother and child is different, but I suppose this is how it's meant to be. We *feel* each other. The love between us is powerful and grounding and yet ever so uplifting.

Keoni, however, witnessed some of the fights between Paul and me. This, I was not proud of. I would hold him in my arms afterward, apologizing and telling him how loved he was. I would try to shift the energy, making him feel loved on many different levels. I often think how horrible we were as parents for allowing him to experience that with us, but I know on a soul level that he chose Paul and me as his parents in this lifetime for a reason. And those experiences served to teach all three of us lessons. I believe that we write experiences into our story to learn from them and further our growth as souls. The best thing I could do as his mother was to continue loving him and doing my best to create a healthier and safer space for him. This also meant learning to love myself more. Although they say parents are here to teach their children, I'd have to say that my child has taught me numerous valuable lessons in regard to a kind of Love way beyond anything I'd ever imagined Love to be.

Regarding my career, as I continued to take hypnotherapy classes to complete my certifications, I saw clients and expanded my spiritual practice. I helped people work on themselves and their own healings. I couldn't believe what I was capable of, and this in turn, increased my confidence and motivation to grow.

In class, we were empowered to work on ourselves in order to learn the different exercises and lesson plans. This perfectly went hand-in-hand with what I was already doing. At times, we paired up with other people and practiced on one another. I met a handful of awesome people in that class who became friends.

I worked quietly on wounds from my past, layer upon layer. The deeper the understanding, the more there was to accept, forgive, make peace with, and to send Love to. I created a blueprint to forgiveness and freedom. It started with understanding oneself, one's role, others, their roles, and the *whole*. Similar to learning to love yourself, you must learn *about* yourself first. Why are you the way you are? Who are you *truly*? Self-knowledge and healing creates places for love to live within you. How could you fully give yourself Love and become that which is Love in its entirety, if you didn't believe you deserved it, if you maintained barriers and defenses against being vulnerable and brave enough to accept it?

To give unconditional love means you have done your due diligence to learn and understand everything about an experience or person and have still chosen to accept and love every bit of them, giving them love even when they've withdrawn from you. I don't mean that you should be a mat people walk all over. No, you're not here to be used for other's selfish needs and benefits. However, you can love without enabling and without people taking advantage of you. Empower others with Love to be their highest and greatest selves. To love means to free them from the confines of their own fears and insecurities. And to be in love is to feel free and invincible. Therefore, when you love, the best thing you can do for someone is allow them freedom. Love *is* freedom. And I realized that's exactly what I craved.

I took the certification course not only to become a hypnotherapist but also to gain tools to help me learn about myself and navigate through certain blocks. The class was a basic understanding of hypnotherapy, energy psychology, and neurolinguistic programming. However, it helped me open other doors to those topics and delve deeper on my own time, with my own work.

The certification course was split into blocks of different topics. We had finished the first block and returned for the second after a two-week break. This time, the classes were held in another location, closer to the coast, in beautiful downtown La Jolla. My friend, Victoria, and I had decided to carpool. As we walked in, we noticed new faces. People who are attracted to non-traditional knowledge fascinate me. They're often unique and open-minded, and it was a fun mystery to figure out who would become a new friend. One person drew my attention with his loud, raspy voice that echoed from the opposite side of the room. With a hint of Southern twang mixed with enthusiasm, I heard him talking about his spiritual practice. Right away, my ears perked up. When I approached him, and as I had speculated, we instantly clicked. (Ironically, I later nicknamed him "Pops," and he became a mentor, who'd also help me work on healing more wounds from my past.)

As we found seats, I noticed another new person who was checking me out. I thought I might know him, but wasn't sure if it was that he looked familiar or that his energy felt familiar. So much is going on psychologically and energetically when we first come in contact with people. They may remind us of someone, or something about them can trigger an unconscious attraction or aversion. In this case, it was the latter. The energy between us each time we glanced at each other felt like an electrical current. I'd never experienced that before. Was it coming from him, from me? Either way, it made me feel uncomfortable, almost like I was being unveiled. I didn't like that, so I made up my mind that I didn't like him. (I know, how immature and backward from everything I believed in and preached.) But undeniably, I felt bothered by him and wanted to cut any kind of energy cord between us right away. It was a strange reaction. I was almost disgusted by his energy, and I couldn't figure out why.

We started class with an ice breaker as usual. The instructor asked a question or named a topic and threw a ball to someone, and that someone either answered the question or replied back with an association and then threw it to someone else, and so on. Someone tossed it to him; he threw it at me, even though I sat on the complete opposite side of the room. I think I almost gave him a mean glare.

After the game, the instructor wanted to go around and have people say their names and talk about their dreams and what they aspired to do. As it came to his turn, he introduced himself as Brian and proceeded to tell the class that he enjoyed traveling and wanted to someday have a farmhouse in the South of France.

A what?! Whoa, buddy, that's *my* dream you just described! How dare you?! I mean it was verbatim: "Someday I'd like to have a farmhouse in the South of France." Not a beach house or a townhouse or a home. No, a FARMHOUSE. Not in France, not in Paris, but specifically the South of France. Who was this guy? That was *my* dream, and he'd totally ripped it off of my dream board at home and from my journals growing up. If I hadn't liked him before, I really didn't like him after he said that.

The following morning, as people arrived at class, I chose a spot and refused to acknowledge Brian as he entered the room and took a seat close by. I ignored him.

"Divine, right? Or is it Grace?"

"Divine's right. You can call me Divine." (Only my close friends called me Grace.)

"How do you know Kayla Geller?"

"Excuse me, but how do you know that I know Kayla Geller?"

"I saw that we both had a Facebook friend in common."

Initially I was livid. Had he just low-key stalked me on Facebook and indirectly admitted to it? I'd thought this well-put-together guy (who let it be known he was a doctor, traveled, vacationed, had a nice home, car, etc.), would be intelligent, with a set of good manners. But no, like a teenage girl, he had explored social media for info. It's interesting how someone who comes off as arrogant and superior can elicit feelings of disgust from those of us whose confidence in ourselves is shaky. There's such a cultural push for material success, that when we meet someone who has achieved that lifestyle of ease, we often overlook the hard work it took to get there. It's so flashy, that when we don't have the same shiny outer container, it's as if an internalized judgmental voice is measuring us against them. Even if we know that those "things" are not what makes a person feel happy or truly rich in spirit. So when we see a flaw in that person, it's a bit of a relief – ah, that person is human too. The standards I'm setting for myself could perhaps be too high for anyone! But good grief, seriously, who did he think he was?

He was Brian. At that moment, I intensely disliked him and was annoyed by his seeming superficiality and self-centered ways. I assumed he was in the crowd who had flocked to the trend of conscious thinking (not so new but right up there next to yoga and green smoothies). However, as time went on, we shared our perspectives on love and adventure. I saw past his image. He was like me, longing for a life of love, passion, depth, and meaning, and I admired that. It is a journey to meld the intellect and the heart, and even though when we met, the material world figured prominently, he became one of my closest friends, someone I trusted and felt safe with. Observing where he was on the path, prompted me to reflect on the concept of surrender—how that underpinning of faith can dissolve the fear of losing status and possessions.

Some months later, for reasons I no longer recall, we had a falling out. It led to a couple months of not speaking. During that time, I finished hypnotherapy certifications and was ready to hang that piece of paper up. Although I rented out office space a couple times a week, I thought it might be time to get an office of my own. Thus began a hefty debate: Do I take the plunge? Just like that? Just do it?! It was crazy brave, was it not? But it resonated, and I had the support of Spirit. As I meditated on it, the energy I received inspired me to go and create. When we make the decision to go after something, to purely create something good from our cores, the Universe always has our backs, and nothing and no one can stop us, except our own selves.

I needed to make sure my intentions were set for my highest and greatest good and also for the good of everyone else. They were: my aspirations were to help more people, and growing my healing practice would help to accomplish exactly that. Check, check, and check. With Spirit behind me, calculations performed, and all the signs pointing me to create, I decided to courageously take my business to the next level. I looked for offices and stumbled upon an ad for one reasonably priced in a hip and trendy part of town. I made an appointment to see it and had my friend Ariel meet me there for moral support.

Ariel and I had met at the bank. We had one of those friendships where it didn't matter how many months or even years has passed, we'd pick up from where we'd left off. I love this kind of friendship because, in order to create it, it needs to be strong and rooted in something way deeper than surface level. We were always present with one another, during beautiful and even some of the crazier moments of our lives.

Ariel was a flamboyant, beautiful butterfly whom everyone loved and gravitated toward when she entered the room. She was awake and consciously on her own journey to delve deeper into truth. We'd compare notes about our detours and inspire each other to grow.

Ariel and I met with the office manager and found out the space would be completely new, as in - it wasn't even finished being built. A salon owner had decided to expand and was creating rooms behind and above the salon to rent out to alternative and holistic practitioners (energy healers, chiropractors, hypnotherapists, massage therapists, etc.). I thought it was a perfect concept and fell in love with it immediately. I told the office manager right away that I was definitely interested and would get back to him when ready to make a definite decision. After a couple days of meditating on it, it was time to let him know that I was in. I was going to say yes to the office!

I made another appointment, this time with the salon owner himself. On my drive down, I randomly looked up toward the sky and noticed a patch of blue where the clouds had opened up, and in that small opening, there was a rainbow. And for some odd reason, I thought of Brian, and my heart longed for peace. I told myself that maybe it was time to call a truce and approach him.

A loud clash of positive energies that exploded upon connection was how I experienced meeting the salon owner. I enjoyed his energy, as it was light and high. He was French, which of course was a plus, considering my being a Francophile.

"Jacques, I'm excited about the office space! And the big picture, your overall vision of what you are building is brilliant! I bet people are booking left and right for spaces here."

"I'm glad you like the space, and my overall goal. I think it's going to be great too. I've had a few practitioners inquire. So far, we have a colonic hydrotherapy practitioner, a couple massage therapists, an acupuncturist, a couple estheticians, and now a hypnotherapist and intuitive- you!"

"Oh wow, that's awesome! What a variety of services you'll have here!"

"Well, I was hoping for a nutritionist, too. That would really complete it! Then you've got mind, spirit, and body, right?!"

"Right...I hear ya!"

"Would you happen to know a nutritionist who's looking for an office? They'll have so much opportunity to grow in this location."

Hmm... do I tell him about Brian? I mean, I know Brian is looking for a new space at the moment, and this would be ideal for him because he's right down the street.

"Uh... yeah, I do know someone who might be interested, in fact."

Yeah, except that he and I are totally not on speaking terms at the moment. But maybe this is a sign that I need to get in touch with Brian, like the rainbow on my drive down. Could that have been a sign from Spirit that it's time to make peace? Clouds are clearing out of our atmosphere to create a rainbow of harmony? Okay, that works. I'll go with that.

"Oh Divine, that would be spectacular! Could you call or text that person now and ask? I would really love it if we can get them to come aboard too!"

"Um, yeah sure. I'll send him a text. It's my friend, Brian. He lives really close."

"Oh that's even better. Maybe he can meet us here, now."

"Oh... now?!"

"I'll wait for him. Why don't you ask him if he's available to meet us here in the next 15 minutes?"

I sent a text. "Hey Brian, I know we haven't talked in a while. Hope you're well. I'm actually just up your street meeting with owner of office space I'm renting. Know you're looking. Owner leasing to holistic/alternative healing practitioners. Might want to check it out. Address is..." *Send! Okay phew, that wasn't so bad, was it, Grace?*

"Alright, I texted my friend, but I'm not sure when I'll hear back from him..."

Ding!

Oh wow... a response already!

"Hey Grace. How long will you be there? I can be there in 10 minutes. Can you wait for me?"

"Yes. I'll still be here. See you soon."

"Perfect. See you soon."

"Oh, he's on his way! He'll be here in 10 minutes!"

"Wow, awesome! I hope he likes the space! This will be perfect if he says yes to it!"

Oh crap, he's really coming. He'll be here soon. Do I pretend like we're in good standing? Do I act like we've been friends forever? Do I give him the cold shoulder? Or maybe I should leave now. Shit. Why am I nervous? It's just Brian...

Upon his arrival, we acted like friends who never had a chasm of silence between them. We conversed with the owner for longer than expected. The energy between us all was light and familiar, and Brian was onboard.

As the owner bid us good night and left for his home on top of the salon, Brian and I were left to confront the awkward energy that had been between us the last couple months. Although it was late, he asked me to take a walk with him. We apologized to one another, and as we hugged it out, it was like the heavens opened up again. He said he never wanted us to lose contact with each other again and that our friendship meant a lot to him.

Listening to him, a cord rang within me. You know those gut responses that go against what you're hoping for? The voice of instinct – so do we listen or bury it...

Chapter 19

Divine Intuitions settled into the heart of Hillcrest. People were curious and interested, and I felt total gratitude and excitement. I didn't know how to fully run my business at this level, but I figured that I'd learn in the process. I was so grateful for Paul's support with my new venture. Had he finally decided to hold the umbrella over me and help since I had held up the umbrella for him as he'd established himself in his dream career? I was grateful and hopeful.

Unfortunately, the emotional distance between us never lessened, and it was time for relationship talk. We communicated that it didn't feel the same anymore, and the best decision might be to go our separate ways since our paths no longer resonated. There were times when we talked about divorce as we held each other in bed. It was mature and sad at the same time. Our fights were no longer verbally-abusive screaming matches. We didn't say anything. It was like the energy of our marriage was dying. I felt for Paul because I knew he was hurting. Whether it was his ego or his heart, it didn't matter. I felt horrible when seeing that, but I was hurting too. And I knew there would be no end to the pain if we continued living together.

Had I fallen out of love with him? I would safely say, yes, I had. But did I still love him? Definitely. In fact, I realized I loved him more than I ever had, but it had a different quality. I wanted him to be happy and to enjoy the kind of love he deserved, even if it meant it wasn't with me.

We acted like roommates at home. There were times when I felt that, in our minds, we had already decided the romantic part of our relationship was over. However, it was our first-year wedding anniversary, so in a last attempt to salvage anything remaining, we decided to celebrate. We flew back to Cabo. Although it was a fun trip, the distance between us was more pronounced, and the lack of connection left us feeling starkly awkward. When we got back from our trip, talks about separation and divorce increased. These talks were matter-of-fact, unemotional. I was sad and scared about how the next few months would unfold, but understood separating was the best thing for us if we wanted to find true happiness.

The next few months, my business grew, and I started seeing 18-20+ clients a week. I was crazy busy, but in a good way. One afternoon, Brian knocked on my door. I sensed a different energy to him.

"Hey Grace, can we sit and talk after our last clients this afternoon?"

"Yeah, sure thing! What's going on? What did you want to talk about? And dude, why so formal about it? You could have just texted me or walked in, the door's open..."

"I'm just being polite. There's something I wanted to talk to you about."

"Alright, fair enough. I appreciate that. I'll see you after 5pm!"

I was weirded out by Brian's distant stance and wondered what he wanted to talk about during the next couple hours.

When it was time, he walked into my office and closed the door behind him which gave me the feeling that whatever he wanted to talk about was more private that usual. He took a seat and sighed deeply.

"Alright dude, so what's going on?"

"I'm not sure if you already know or have felt my energy lately, but I wanted to let you know that it dawned on me that I have feelings for you, feelings beyond friendship level."

"Ohhhh... okay..." *Oh man, is he really telling me this?*

"I just wanted to be open and honest about the way I feel. There's nothing that needs to be done about this realization. I think I just need to work through my emotions."

"Well, what do you mean, there's nothing that needs to be done about this… as if there's ever anything that needs to be done about one's feelings?" *I am so confused right now. What's his intention here? Why is he telling me this now?*

"I mean, well, we shouldn't do anything about it. You're about to be separated and divorced. I don't want to make things more complicated for you than they already are, and we're friends, so that's that."

"Well, yeah, and I don't know how I feel about this right now, you telling me you have feelings for me. It's just a lot right now."

"Exactly, and it would be wrong to do anything about it now considering the situation you're in. I wanted to let you know that I'll be taking some time to process through these feelings. We don't have to talk about it anymore after today."

"Okay, yeah."

"I care about our friendship and I don't want to lose you as a friend."

"Ditto. I don't want to hurt our friendship either."

Great, one more area of confusion to add to the mix.

With my hectic schedule and the things I was trying to process in my head regarding Paul and I, I lost clarity and control when it came to my business. It was time to leave my office and close my practice temporarily while I dealt with my soon-to-be separation and divorce.

I remember the last morning I woke up in our bed, in the home Paul and I shared. I felt empty. A part of me wanted to throw a blanket around me and Paul and keep us safe from the hurt about to rain down upon us. A part of me wanted to stay. But I also knew that staying would only be a temporary fix. I wanted to be happy, once and for all, and I wanted him to be happy, too. I wished we could have had a never-ending kind of happiness, but this was not the place we would find it, not with each other. Looking back at our relationship, since he had held on to his prior love, his heart had never opened wide enough to receive the fullness of my love, nor had it healed to free him to reciprocate. And ultimately, I withdrew the entirety of my loving heart.

Though it may appear selfish, walking away from a marriage that felt rife with barriers to closeness, was a *self-loving* action. I finally chose honoring myself over loving him. Is that really selfish? Yes, I suppose it is in a way. But it wasn't bad. All my life I had been selfless, putting myself second, and for once I wanted to come first. Even though I knew the price would be discomfort and pain, for who knew how long, before I became truly happy. And it turned out that the following months would be the toughest in my life.

I left our home that morning with a bag of clothes and headed for my father's home. This was one of the hardest things I had ever done—walk away from someone I loved. Allow someone to hurt in order to give him the happiness he deserved. Rouse him from this fake white-picket-fenced world, to awaken in the cold reality of brokenness and hurt. I had always fought for love; this time it looked like I was doing the complete opposite. In reality, though, I was loving more than I ever had.

As I settled into my father's house, adjusting to a verbal agreement of 50/50 custody of Keoni, it quickly became obvious we needed a place of our own, especially one where I could have solitude and create a safe space to process and heal. Without planning things out, I looked for apartments based on wishful thinking. I didn't know how I was going to do it. I had no money and no real job, as I'd put a temporary pause on running my business full time. I had nothing. In fact, I was in the negative. Everything I had saved up for and bought to furnish my first home: my sofa, bed, plates, cups, utensils, sheets, towels, wall décor, and so much more, I left at *his* house. I didn't want to take it with me, and I didn't want anything else from him, period. I wanted peace between us and thought that maybe if I didn't leave him in an empty house it would help with easing into this new reality. He hurt anyway. I gave up a lot, and in turn, I hurt just as much if not more.

The situation between us was permanent. There was no getting back together like before. While apartment shopping, I met a charming French man. It was a month after my separation, and surprisingly, I allowed myself to get involved romantically. I knew that what I was doing was avoiding emotions and thoughts I needed to process. Being human, I chose a distraction. It was too painful to look at what was in front of me. Another part was perhaps to seal my separation from Paul as official and done. And lastly, I wasn't thinking clearly. I was smack dab in the middle of a horrible experience and could not ground myself for the life of me. Looking back, this decision to date someone else right away was not a good idea. It hurt Paul even more, which in turn, hurt me more and prolonged the work I needed to do on myself in solitude. It was a good thing this ran a short course. Even so, it did include a great deal of lessons.

He was French, so I'll call him *Frenchy* (since that was how Brian and other friends referred to him). He was definitely an interesting guy– charming, dressed up in a handsome suit all the time, and an artist. I admired him for being brave enough to travel across the pond and move to the U.S. on his own. Everything else about him was dirty, dishonest, and fake. I found out he had cheated on his then fiancée with me. I didn't feel good about that at all. But he was good at creating stories and buttering people up. I caught him in a bunch of lies and ended it. It felt so good to get rid of something so awful, so fast. I wrote his ex-fiancée a letter to apologize and let her know I would not have continued seeing him if I had known the truth—that he was *still* engaged! Emilia and I met up for coffee. She was genuinely heartbroken, and I was part of it, albeit unknowingly. I felt horrible and wanted to humbly apologize and make peace in person. I genuinely cared about connecting with her to offer her truth and some kind of healing. It felt good to do that for me, and I hope it helped her, too.

Meanwhile, Keoni and I were still sleeping on my sister's bedroom floor on an air mattress at my dad's house. As months went by, I felt suffocated with emotions and thoughts I tried suppressing. I was sad. I was *really* sad. I felt guilty. I was terrified. I felt lost and overwhelmed. I was angry. But mostly, I was sad. So many emotions ran through me; I didn't know which to look at first. I was spiraling down quickly. And all I had was myself. I didn't want to tell my friends (or anyone for that matter), how bad I was feeling. Maybe I didn't want them to think I had made the wrong decision. I knew that wasn't the case, I just wasn't a fan of what it came with. I missed my home and my own space. It was quite humbling sleeping on the floor.

Many nights I cried myself to sleep. I missed seeing my son every day. I missed cuddling with him every night before bed. I missed him, period, even though I saw him fifty percent of the time. He was my light, my saving grace. When with him, my heart could come up for a few breaths of fresh air. We giggled, sang, and cuddled as always, and those moments definitely saved me at that time. The thought of my son empowered me to not give up. I questioned if I had failed him, but reminded myself that moving through these trials was especially for *him*. I needed to create a safe space for him to thrive in, one filled with love. I needed to continue putting in the work to make that happen. I felt confident that someday he'd understand why it was the way it was. But being apart half the time was the greatest price paid to move into alignment with a more authentic future for us all.

Chapter 20

There was no backing out. My son had taught me about Love in the deepest and most majestic sense, and I needed to do right by him and prove the validity of that truth.

Love was all I had at that point. It allowed me to hold onto the kind of faith that had cushioned rock bottom in the past. There I was again, and everything, I mean *everything*, hurt. But I wasn't going to let my fears nor the pain stop me from continuing on. I mustered up some courage to get up from the ground, dusted my knees off, and pretended like it didn't hurt...until it didn't. It was like the last stretch of a long run on a scorching day. One foot in front of the other although fatigue demanded I stop and accept defeat. I would not yield. Instead, I remembered who I was. And like an awakened giant, I was a force to be reckoned with. I allowed my world to break apart completely in order to put it back together as it should have been, stronger and more flexible so it would never break again.

God, where are you? Universe, listen up. Spirit, hear me out. Ascended Masters, I speak to you. Angels, behold. I have come to my feet, and need you as my army to guide me along the way while I trudge through this, like the valiant soul that I am. I Am here. I Am that which I AM. And I Am awake and ready.

For four months I allowed myself to hurt, to indulge in this misery, to play victim, to feel weak. I'd let myself be human, and although that is usually a beautiful thing (being human), I was over it. I felt the power of my intentions like an explosion ready to be felt in all the lands, from here to the different worlds beyond. I was not going to stop until I had manifested what I wanted, what I deserved: peace, happiness, and Love. My son would reap the benefits.

As I mentioned earlier, my spiritual perspective was that Keoni had chosen me to be his mother in this life, and it was my responsibility to help him experience Love. So far I had shown him what life looked like when fear and insecurities took control. I wanted him to see what life was like when real Love was present. To show him what this brave Love was capable of. Growing and healing was for me, yes, but also for my son - to honor and thank him for waking me up. When he'd entered my life, I'd started the journey back to truth after being lost and broken. Here I was, lost and broken again. This time, though, the thought of him inspired me so much more. I needed to get back to my truth.

My truth is Love, and this is my story. It was time to once again consciously direct the flow of my story. I had made things happen before; I knew I could make *this* happen. I knew I had to see clients again full time, to help others, but first I needed to put myself together and create a home. I didn't know how I was going to do this because I had literally nothing but my clothes and books. I barely had money in the bank, and I didn't have enough money coming in. I didn't want alimony or child support from Paul, nor anything from anyone but the Universe. I didn't need it because I was capable of standing on my two feet and being able to create. It was the stubborn and independent (and maybe even prideful) side of me that took the reins of this determination.

First, I looked for a full-time job. I knew this was temporary, a stepping stone so to speak, to help me get on my way. After some time searching, I found a job with enough flexibility in time and hours to accommodate me as a single parent. It paid enough and provided benefits. It was perfect! I interviewed and fell in love with the energy of the place. As I left, I felt good about it and told myself that I would indeed be working there. The following week, though, I was disappointed to receive an email from the director telling me that, unfortunately, I had not gotten the position. I emailed back and kindly thanked him for his time.

I felt deflated after learning I hadn't gotten the job. Disappointment and self-doubt crept in that evening. I felt my heart become heavy as I fell asleep hoping for a miracle.

The next morning, I sat down and proclaimed to the Universe that I'd had enough of my current situation. I knew I needed to shift the energy. I closed my eyes and went into meditation. At first, I took a look at myself and what I needed to shift in energy about myself that would match the energy of that which I wanted to create in my reality. For the rest of the manifesting work, I visualized in complete detail what I wanted to bring into my world. I proclaimed that I wanted that exact position that I had interviewed for. I didn't care that I had just received a rejection letter for that job; I knew I had the power within me to shift energy and create. I continued along with my proclamation. I wanted a new car I'd feel safe in (my car was breaking down), a new home for me and my son, a savings account that would afford me a cushion and the ability to buy furniture (little by little), and lastly, peace. I wanted *peace* in my world.

I cried and I shouted toward the Universe, toward Source, toward God, toward Spirit, toward my Angels, toward the Masters, with love and a powerful force that demanded a shift in energy. I felt my whole body warm up and tingle. I was definitely moving something inside of me, thus shifting the energy as a whole in my world. I realized my power, and I used it with the full force of that which it is in its entirety: love. As I started to slowly breathe in and breathe out, calming my breath, wiping my tears away. I gave gratitude to those

I had summoned for their constant presence, especially during my heaviest of times, and for never forsaking me. I knew I was in good hands and I felt safe. I had reconnected with my faith. With a little bit of grace, I came back to my truth for that one moment in order to change moments to come in my life forever.

As I closed out my meditation, still wiping tears off my cheeks, I noticed I had missed a call during my meditation. I listened to the voicemail right away. It was the director with whom I had interviewed, who had emailed me the rejection letter. Apparently, something had come up, and they needed another person to fill the position. He offered me the job and wanted to welcome me into the company if I was still interested in working for them. As soon as the message ended, I started to cry. Could my meditation, my proclamation into the Universe, have been that strong, that loud, that powerful? My faith, my God, Spirit, my protectors, they had never forsaken me before, why would they start now? And here they were, once again confirming every bit of *knowing* I'd ever felt throughout my life. This was a turning point. I had changed the game. The outcome was up to me now, as it always had been without my awareness. I'd shifted the energy, just like that. It was like magic; it *was* magic.

That was only Tuesday. There were more items on my list that I needed to manifest into my reality and more days left in the week, and even month. I wasn't done yet. I was my own Master, ready to create.

Friday evening, I fell asleep talking to my Angels, praying to them, particularly to Archangel Raphael. I asked for assistance in manifesting the other items on my list. I needed to get rid of my car. It was not safe to drive, and I didn't have the money to fix it. I needed to find a home, one I could afford, that would allow me to rebuild a new foundation for Keoni and me. And lastly, I asked again for healing and peace. I didn't want to hurt anymore. I wished for this for everyone involved.

The following Saturday evening as I sat at my sister's desk journaling, my dad handed me an envelope. *Mail, probably another bill. I'll pay when I can.* I was about to tear it up, knowing they'd send it again, when I noticed the envelope was lined with emerald green, Archangel Raphael's color. I stared at the envelope a little longer. *Hmm, certified mail, from my old mortgage company.* Curious, I quickly opened it and pulled out a check for a hefty amount made out to me. It was a payment resulting from an independent foreclosure review done on my home some years ago. *What? It's been years since I foreclosed on my home. And this amount! It's definitely bigger than the usual checks people get from unlawful foreclosures.* To be sure, I investigated the claim and where it came from. There was a phone number that I called to confirm the check's legitimacy. It was real!

The amount would more than help me get back up on my two feet. It was enough to afford me peace of mind. I was in awe and almost in disbelief. But I knew this was a blessing from the Universe.

A few days later, after doing some research, I traded in my car. It was a good deal, and it saved me a lot of money, considering the amount I would have spent trying to fix it. *Wow, I'm on a roll, but I'm not done yet. Let's keep going. Onto the next item on my list.* I meditated every day, sometimes even a few times a day, focusing on those things I intended to manifest and sending gratitude for the blessings I had received the prior week. My life was about to turn around. I could feel debris from the explosion of an old life starting to settle, and a new life emerging.

I had a new car I felt safe in. I had a job that served as a stepping stone until I could see clients again. With money coming in, I was building up a brand new savings account to help create my new foundation. I was still in search for a home, though.

Everything I found in the area where I wanted to settle

was above my price range. The ones I could afford were located in areas I didn't care for. So I sat down in meditation and focused solely on a vision of my ideal home. I envisioned the ideal location and details of the home. It needed at least two bedrooms, to be clean, to have good energy, and to be affordable (at least $500 less than the average rental in my preferred location).

A couple days later, as I searched again for the 100th time, I saw a listing for a two-bedroom, two-bath home, freshly repainted, re-carpeted, and redone for the next tenants. It was located in the exact location I was looking for. And the best part about it was that it was listed for $500 less than other rentals in the area. *How perfect! But what's the catch?!* I quickly called and made an appointment to see the condo in the next hour.

As I walked in, the first thing I noticed was how bright it was. The sun naturally brightened the home, and the energy inside felt light and cheery. I spoke with the landlords' aunt who was present in lieu of the landlords, since they lived out of state. Her energy felt warm and welcoming. As I toured the condo, I felt it resonate. This home was exactly what I was looking for. There was no catch. It was going for the listed price, and there was nothing more to it. I immediately told her that I'd take it. I left her an application, and the next day, I was contacted by the two landlords to set up a phone interview. As I spoke with them that evening, it felt like speaking to two friends. We laughed and connected easily. Within 24 hours, they contacted me to let me know they'd chosen me to be their tenant, and I could move in the following week.

Was it really that simple? Within three weeks' time, I had manifested specific life necessities that I had asked for. Ironically, my son and I moved in the day after Thanksgiving. I felt complete gratitude for the help I had received from the Universe, from God, from my Angels, from Spirit, and from the Ascended Masters. Once again, my faith had created magic in my life, magic, because everything miraculously fell into place without a real logical explanation for the timeline of events, except for the work that I had put in during meditations. It validated that I had made the right decision to move on from an old life and that I was again being divinely guided.

The rest of what I had proclaimed to the Universe that I wanted to manifest and create in my world was up to me. They had helped create the space I needed to work on the healing and peace I had asked for. I diligently went to work to clean house, my spiritual house, in order to start to heal.

In the next couple of months, I created a warm and loving home for me and my son. I did the work to lighten the energy in our space. Doors and windows were kept open, allowing sun to fill the home with light. I asked the Angels to come in and serve as protectors, to foster love in its lightest, purest, and most beautiful form. Little by little, we put our home together. The loving, peaceful energy was felt by welcome guests that gravitated to it, some staying longer than expected. Each time they left, I cleared the energy and lightened it up even more.

I saw clients after work and during the weekends. It felt good to be helping people again. Every one of my clients walked in and gained clarity, peace, healing, and love, before his or her departure. For years, this had been exactly the kind of home I'd wanted to create.

Around this time, Paul and I finalized our divorce. We walked into the courthouse together, signed the papers, and turned them in. We walked out high-fiving one another and grabbed pizza and beer to celebrate a moment of coming full circle in our journey. We were somewhat at peace. I knew he was still processing and even hurting; I was too, but the waters between us were fairly calm on the surface.

I vividly remember a day soon after—a unique day of conscious clarity inspired by Keoni. His majesty (my son), and I were enjoying a lazy Saturday morning that turned into the afternoon, lying around on the floors of our apartment. His giggles echoed in my ear. I felt his joy in my heart and melted into his gentle, sweet touch and found all the riches of the world in that small moment. It felt so complete, both of us bathed in love. I wished I could keep him by my side, in my embrace, under my loving guidance *forever*. Couldn't we just stay here—in the ether of innocence and purity—and forget the rest of the world?

Life paused and I, for once, felt in awe of how beautiful the stillness was.

I reflected on how, after fighting for so long against the flow, I had surrendered by stepping into my power the day I spoke directly to every Divine source I was aware of. I felt grateful for the journey, for what it had entailed- the beautiful, the ugly, and the in-between, and for where it had taken me. Gazing upon my beautiful baby boy, I felt gratitude for the peace that embraced our presence and stilled us, revealing the true nature of life and our beings, strong and powerful yet delicate and filled with so much love. I felt grateful for the perfection of being able to share that magical moment with him. In that instant I recognized what life was about, what it meant to be fully present. Keoni helped awaken me to this truth, and it forever changed our lives for the better. I will always be grateful for the role my son played and continues to play in my life.

I knew the future would provide other adventures; battles to fight; hurt and pain to experience, process, and heal; more growth to gain; insight to learn; and work to do. But in that moment I knew that, yes, the peace and love I had sought my entire life – was real. And there it was, making its way into existence in my life. Another wink from the Universe that I was on the right path. Challenges need not daunt me. Whenever I needed to, I could return to or create this foundation of love and peace.

The coming new year would mark a time when I fully indulged my lifelong desire for freedom. Right before the year began, I wrote a letter to "him," whomever *he* would turn out to be, the man I would share the remainder of my life with, who I knew would empower me to go after my purpose and passion. In the letter, I said I was ready to fully delve into working on myself, and he could start searching for me. The day he'd find me, I'd be ready. I intuitively knew that it wouldn't be long. From messages in my meditations and dreams, I knew he would enter my life the following year. In the meantime, I was to continue inner work and encourage myself to be brave and adventurous. I had longed for ultimate freedom and independence, ever since I fell in love with solitude as a child. Complete liberation from an old life and the thrill of the adventures of a soul set on fire by passion awaited my ignition; I dared not let it wait any longer…

Chapter 21

France had called to me my entire life, and here I was, planning a trip. A part of me felt like I was going home even though I had never been there. The South of France was the place of mysteries I had curiously explored regarding Jesus and Mary Magdalene (the Patron Saint of France), and also, perhaps, connected to part of my soul. This natural affinity for the area, as well as my past life regression experience, supported my belief that the trip would help uncover truth within myself to guide me to peace. I wasn't sure what that might entail or what I would discover, but I knew it was going to happen.

For months before my trip, I sat in meditation and asked for guidance from the Ascended Masters, the Angels, and Source, to show me where to go and what to do. To be guided by Spirit, I based all decision-making on my gut feeling-whether or not it *felt* good. I needed to make sure it *felt* right deep inside. I was not making plans by logic alone. This was a spiritual adventure; therefore, I wanted to follow the promptings of my intuition and heart. I was to fly into Paris, and as soon as I arrived take the train down to the South of France. After debating many times over which city to stay in, I decided to make Marseille my base city. From there, I'd visit other cities in the South of France by train, bus, or car. Two days before coming back to the States, I'd travel north to explore Paris.

One random Tuesday morning, I put my procrastination aside and decided to be brave about it. Although Brian and I had spoken numerous times about traveling to France together (we had remained close friends), he was still in indecision mode, while I felt a growing urgency to go. I didn't want to wait for him any longer. *Maybe this trip is for me to experience alone.*

That morning, I found flights that were a lot less expensive than any previous flights I had seen posted.

Should I book now? Am I really doing this? Can I really manage to go on my own? I mean, what if the prices drop even more tomorrow or the next day or the day after that? No, I can't think that way. I need to just do it now. Okay...I'm booking my flights. Yes, I'm going to France!

I was committed. Once word got around of my upcoming trip, several family members and friends feared for my safety. Most joked about the movie *Taken* with Liam Neeson. Even Paul joked about it. I never bought into any of those fears and doubts. I knew I would be taken care of. I would not only be safe and protected, but I knew I'd be divinely guided to explore and discover what it was that awaited me.

I couldn't afford hotels or any type of fancy lodging, so I decided to look on Airbnb and TripAdvisor for a private room. As I flipped through possibilities on the websites, one attracted my attention. Although it didn't have any reviews and didn't seem like it was anything grand or fancy (simply a private room in a family's home), it felt good to me. I knew I had to stay there. If I had told others that this lodging had no reviews and was a room in a home with a family that barely spoke English, they probably would have tainted the energy with fear and doubt. I felt positively about it. I trusted that I needed to stay with them for reasons I couldn't yet explain.

I messaged back and forth with the lady who had listed the place regarding the details of my arrival and questions about my stay. Her name was Nesrine. She lived in the house with her family: Ahmed her husband, her two youngest kids, Safia and Hamid; and her oldest daughter, Ines, who came home on weekends from college in the nearby city, Aix En Provence. Our interaction via email, was initially a bit challenging due to the language barrier, but as time went by, I felt a huge amount of kindness radiating from her being. I intuitively knew I would be safe staying with them.

The only thing that pulled at my heartstrings and saddened me was that I wasn't going to see my son for two weeks. This would be the longest time I had ever been away from him. I knew it would be okay considering Paul had agreed to help me chat with Keoni over Google Hangouts. We could talk and see each other's faces on my computer screen. Hopefully, this would lessen the sting of missing him.

Yes, I was planning to cross the ocean for spiritual lessons specific to my journey, but quite frankly, there were plenty at home. Paul had recently started seeing a girl named Tara. She seemed to be his dream girl: similar hobbies, interests, passions, and even personality traits. Everything he had been looking for, and she was able to love him in the way he needed and wanted to be loved. I knew he was on his way to a happy place, and this made me happy for him. They say when you love someone, you want nothing but happiness for that person, even if it means it will not be shared with you. I'd arrived at that place, genuinely glad for them.

I adjusted to the situation and felt excited to hear of this new relationship, and I looked forward to meeting her. Unfortunately, I didn't believe that she was too excited about me. Understandably, Paul's perspective, likely colored by his experience of our separation, probably didn't paint me in the best light. Pretty common dynamics in a situation such as ours, and though tough to get off on a defensive start, I tried to stay open-hearted.

As their relationship evolved, I noticed Tara begin to assert herself more as a maternal figure for my son, and even began speaking on Paul's behalf on matters regarding Keoni. She began volunteering at Keoni's school at a time when my work schedule wouldn't afford me the opportunity to do so. During that time, parents, teachers, and classmates assumed she was Keoni's mom. I began to feel marginalized in my son's life. I didn't feel better about the situation when I learned they were encouraging Keoni to call Tara, "Mommy" and refer to me as "Grace" or "Mama Grace" when he was at their house. This was particularly surprising in light of past conversations with Paul who had expressed feeling uncomfortable when we saw acquaintances do that very thing. It was as if I was in a competition I hadn't signed up for.

I felt hurt by this. It's common knowledge that children need to feel positively about both of their parents; it's less stressful for them and it builds their self-esteem. I cared that my son had a good relationship with his father, separate from the one I had with Paul. I went out of my way to praise him to my son, referred to him as "Papa," and encouraged Keoni to show him respect. I rarely believed that sentiment was reciprocated, and at times, thought the opposite may have been true. A few times I expressed my concerns, but those conversations were never particularly productive.

Quite the situation to assess one's connection to one's own power! And mine wasn't robust. Here I was, putting energy into creating a healthy and peaceful life, working hard to sustain myself and my son, and actively working to heal from the past, and yet, I realized I was still under Paul's emotional control. How my relationship with Keoni was perceived in his household mattered to me. Ideally, we'd be positive and supportive when co-parenting, but communication and actions remained as they had when we'd been married, and it was probably unrealistic to expect anything different.

So I felt despondent and at times slipped into believing that I was horrible. I worried that engaging Paul to ensure we were on equal footing would lead to conflict, which would ultimately hurt my son. I didn't want to build up negative energy that would, in turn, hurt Keoni. I focused inward and only spoke up if I thought a situation was particularly egregious. Even if Paul didn't appreciate or acknowledge it, I often felt I met him more than half way to keep the peace.

This area of my life provided the type of painful spiritual lessons that stretch us deep into our hearts to connect with our own sense of a competent, lovable self. They provided me with opportunities for growth, pushing me to remain strong as an example of love. What mattered was my son's acknowledgement of me, not Paul's, nor anyone else's. Just Keoni's.

Over the years, little by little, Paul, Tara and I have made considerable strides in working together peacefully. Although it's a work in progress, I will forever be grateful to Tara for loving and caring for my son when Keoni stays with them. Likewise, when speaking with Keoni, I will continue referring to Paul as an awesome dad.

Amidst all this, I, on the other hand, was open to dating and getting to know people as well but didn't want to fully commit to anything. I was indulging in my independence. I started spending time with a man who I had actually met working at the bank years ago.

I'll be honest, I was so surprised to learn that he was on a spiritual journey, especially because of my brief interactions with him in the past. But that's just it, we should never judge or make assumptions about people, because we never know what a person is going through or who they are behind closed doors. We spent a little time together – it's a treat to share interactions with people on a similar path - but my original instincts proved correct. The relationship didn't develop too much before it broke off.

That's another thing I've learned, when I listen to that quiet, instinctual voice, the information I receive can be trusted. I don't know why it's so hard for us to hear the warnings – not only about possible serious problems that can arise, but the simple knowing: this is not right for me, nice guy, not the right fit. What a lot of heartbreak and time we'd save, if we trusted that voice and knew the Universe had a better romantic plan in store for us.

Admittedly, what that voice is advising is not always crystal clear. For instance, my friendship with Brian had grown throughout the previous two years. I enjoyed daily, good morning texts usually accompanied by an inspirational meme or idea; messages throughout the day; and good night text messages. We didn't see each other often; we hung out only here and there. We didn't need to, though, because we were always in communication, sharing, empowering one another to go after our dreams. We had each other's backs. And after I'd dismissed his feelings the year before, I'd thought we'd moved past that.

I treasured his friendship because it is a gift to feel safe enough to reveal one's true self, and we had conquered the fear of not being enough, the fear of lacking perfection, the fear of being rejected. It is a relief to be authentically ourselves with another. But when both people aren't on the same page as far as their feelings for each other go…then the harmonious relationship is in jeopardy.

Suffice it to say, the possibility of a romantic relationship came close to fruition, but I got scared. When friends consider changing their relationship, it can be confusing, with so much at stake. Even when we looked at each other and I felt the energy change, I didn't know if I could trust his intentions, nor was I in a place to move forward if they were "honorable." For a few months, we'd move closer, then away from each other. Then I felt his spirit, energy and presence slowly leaving. This deeply saddened me. Although we still communicated, a part of him was disengaging, and I felt utterly abandoned. I missed my friend.

At that point, I wished there was no such thing as *feelings*, because *feelings* had shaken things up and broken them apart. I wished I had never felt for him. Maybe then it would have been safe for us to continue being friends. Was this my fault? Had I hoped for too much? Or maybe not hoped enough? Should I have been braver and proclaimed how I really felt? *How did I really feel? Did I even know?* See how confusing this can get! Whether it was one of those explanations or one of another million what-ifs, it needed to happen as it did to bring me where I am today, even if that meant he was no longer in my life.

As I prepared to depart for France, a part of me longed for Brian to be by my side. I wished that he had decided to come along. And...I had to acknowledge that a natural relationship evolved smoothly, without a cloud of confusion hampering its flow. I would trust what I was told by intuitive friends and messages in my meditation: when I returned from France, I would at last be with the person I was to spend the rest of my life with. I believed this, and knew it was going to happen.

My mind and spirit left that romantic prophesy behind and aligned with the present. A truth more powerful than any other I'd known was on the horizon. My courage was buoyed by direct calls unto the Angels, the Ascended Masters, and God to keep me safe along the way. Whatever purpose there was for me in France, let it be carried out!

I was to fly from San Diego to Chicago for a layover and then off to Paris. And from Paris, I would take the train down to Marseille. And stay there for eight days. I didn't have much money to spend, but I knew it would be enough. I had worked hard the last couple months saving for this trip, seeing endless clients after my day job and during the weekends. It had been exhausting, but I'd needed to do it. The Universe had sent me client upon client upon client to help make this work.

The night before I left, I dropped off Keoni at Paul's. I gave him a big hug and a handful of kisses. I promised that I would chat with him and see him on the computer screen as soon as I got to France. I felt so sad leaving. And a bit scared. What if this was the last time I'd ever see him? What if something bad happens to me in France? I probably shouldn't go. What if I get stuck there? Ahhhh! My mind was freaking out. A fearful mindset attempted to get a hold of me the last minute before I left. I quickly shook it off. No, I was going to France. I was going to France alone... and I was going to LOVE it.

Chapter 22

I arrived at the airport early, out of excitement. I read a book and waited patiently to board the plane.

"Our flight leaving for Chicago, will be delayed by 45 minutes," came an announcement over the loud speaker.

What? Oh no! I don't want to miss my flight to Paris from Chicago and then, miss my train to Marseille. I can't afford to miss any flights or train reservations!

When we were able to board, I was glad to discover my seat was near the entrance of the plane. I conversed with the two people I sat with.

"So is Chicago pretty much your final destination?" I inquired of my seatmates.

"I'm headed to New York, actually."

"Yeah, I'm headed to Newark to visit some friends in New Jersey."

"Oh nice, seems like we're all needing to get to a connecting flight after this. I'm headed to Paris. I just hope I make my connecting flight…."

"It sounds like you'll only have a few minutes to run to your next flight. It'll be tight. I hope you make it."

"Yeah, I hope so too," I said and explained my situation.

"Wow, so what's in the South of France? Why are you travelling there? Sounds exciting…"

"Well, I'm kind of on a spiritual adventure. I don't really know what's there, but I know there's something waiting for me…"

I continued to talk about feeling drawn to that area of the

world. They were entertained with my stories and understood why it was so important for me to get to France. There was a lady a couple seats back who was also supposed to be on my next flight. She was meeting her family, who were coming from other destinations, then they'd travel to Paris together from O'Hare Airport. In fact, it seemed like there were a handful of us that needed to make the same connecting flight.

The flight attendants made another announcement. "Ladies and Gentlemen, we regret to inform you that we'll be delayed for a total of an hour. However, upon landing, we will allow passengers who have to make connecting flights to get off the plane first. Thank you."

No! This was more terrible news, because it meant I'd have less than 10 minutes to get from one end of the airport to the other before the next flight took off! I was wearing heeled boots and carried my purse and laptop bag. I'd need a miracle to make this happen. *Okay,* I told myself, *as soon as I get off the plane, I'm gonna book like the wind.*

As soon as they opened the doors, people began standing up and crowding the aisles. My two seatmates, one standing on her seat, shouted as loudly as they could, "Attention everyone, clear the way for her. She needs to get off the plane NOW! She needs to make her connecting flight!" I looked back only to give a look of gratitude. I was the second person off that plane.

I bolted. I ran as fast I could through the crowded gates of the airport. Trying to remember directions to my next gate, I mindfully looked up at signs. *Oh, my God, I hope I'm going the right way!* I kept running. My purse was annoying. My laptop bag was heavy. *Please don' let me fall or slip on the floor! What was I thinking, wearing high-heeled boots?* I had one thing on my mind: France. *I have to make this flight.* I ran down and up a tunnel-like thing, back up toward some escalators, and past a handful of gates. *There it is!* I ran toward the doorway. *Oh no! They've just closed the gate.*

As I caught my breath, I explained, "I'm supposed to be boarding this flight. Look, here's my boarding pass. Our flight was an hour late from San Diego. There are more of us coming!"

"I'm sorry. They've closed the gate door. It's too late. You can catch a later flight."

"No, I can't do that! I have to catch a train as soon as I arrive in Paris. If I don't make this flight, I'll miss my train and I *really* can't afford to book new tickets. I'm sorry, I can't take no for an answer. I *need* to be on that plane!"

As they were about to tell me no again, a man who looked like he was part of the crew, but didn't seem familiar to them, came out from the gate doors and asked what was going on. The plane was getting ready to leave, but for some reason this mystery attendant decided to walk out of it to see what was going on.

"I have to get on the plane; I don't care that the gates are closed. Please. I showed up. I did my part. I did the work to be here, to be here now."

He empathized with me.

"Allow her on the plane," he told the airline attendants. "She'll be the last person we'll let on."

Unfortunately, the other passengers from my last flight wouldn't make this connecting flight. The airline personnel reluctantly followed the mystery man's orders. As I made my way to board the plane, I looked back and noticed that the guy had vanished. He couldn't even be spotted outside of the crowd. He was gone, just like that. I felt he was my saving grace. Maybe he was one of the Ascended Masters in disguise helping me on my way, as they are known to do every so often. Regardless of who that guy was, he had helped me tremendously, and I was on my way to France.

My seat was located at the very back of the aircraft. A couple had traded seats with me so they could sit together; I had the last row of seats to myself. I could rest easy. As I settled in, the flight attendant came by.

"Hey, congratulations for making it! We're missing a handful more, but you made it! Why'd you need to get on the plane so badly? You could have caught a later flight, you know," he said.

I explained about the connections and needing to get to Marseilles.

"What's happening there?" he asked.

"I've always dreamed of going to the South of France. It's been calling me for years. I have a good feeling that something there will help me piece together the mystery of *me, my purpose in life*. I've waited all my life for this."

He paused and looked at me in wonder. "Wow! Your life is so romantic and adventurous. I wish mine was like that. It sounds like you're going there for love?"

"In a sense, yes!" *For the Love of the Self, that is.*

"Whatever it is that's calling you to France must be really important. We had to reopen the doors just for you. If you hadn't been so determined, you wouldn't be sitting here right now. I say, good luck to you and to your quest. You're quite a brave little one, going alone, and I hope you find whatever it is or whoever it is that you're looking for."

I hoped so too. Meanwhile, it was time to relax, get comfy, and hopefully fall asleep for the nine-hour flight to Paris.

For sleeping on a plane, I had a remarkably deep, rejuvenating slumber. All that running to make my flight wore me out.

I remember the instant I woke up. We were flying above France, soon to land at Charles de Gaulle Airport. I slid open the hard window shade and sipped the coffee the flight attendant had given me. And then, there she was, standing in all her glory: La Tour D'Eiffel.

The moment I saw the Eiffel Tower, chills ran up and down my spine, as the rush of adrenaline woke me up faster than the coffee I sipped. *I'm home.* Energy warmed my body and moved my gut. All sorts of emotional cords were being rung. I could hear spirit whisper, "Welcome home, child. Welcome home." I knew my soul had lived here before. The energy that it came with, the familiarity at soul level, I knew I'd find what I was looking for that would propel me into the kind of life I had been told time and time again I'd live: one rich with peace, love, bliss, and freedom.

My journey wasn't over when my plane landed. I needed to grab my luggage, get through customs, and find the train to Marseilles. It was easier than I'd thought it would be. And as I finally found the train station in the airport, I was relieved to see I had a couple hours before my train would arrive.

I sat there impatiently, watching the numbers on the board and the time change for arrivals and departures. After a while, I wasn't sure if I was reading the board correctly. After getting the intuitive pull to stand up and ask someone about my train reservations and the times on the board, I mustered up some courage, and with ticket in hand, approached someone.

"Excuse me. Am I in the right place?" I asked a man who looked approachable.

He looked at my ticket. "Oh, your train is arriving now!"

"It is?! Where do I need to go to board the train?"

He didn't even answer, but motioned me to follow him as he grabbed my luggage, leaving the building, and descending down some escalators. As soon as we set foot on the bottom level, my train arrived. Perfect timing.

"That was close. Almost missed it!" he said, smiling.

"Yes! I would have missed it if it wasn't for your help! Thank you so much! Merci beaucoup, monsieur!"

Here was another random individual who'd helped me get on with my journey. I felt like Spirit was continuously coming down into the physical in disguise to guide me along the way. The synchronistic play-by-play of this felt more than mere coincidence.

Sitting on the train, traveling from Paris to the South of France, I felt powerful. I'd made it. I'd won over my doubts. I felt safe. I felt like there was an invisible presence leading me to where I needed to be. I stared out the window, admiring the countryside. France was so beautiful. The further we travelled away from the city, the greener and more picturesque it looked. I read my books and meditated, making sure not to miss my stop. I reveled in my current state of being and quietly celebrated the fact that I was there. Although it had felt like an adventure already (trying to make my flight and my train), I knew there was so much more to come.

It took a few hours before we arrived in Marseilles. I felt excited as I gathered my stuff.

I exited the train and the second my foot touched the platform, it hit me. *Oh my God, what kind of fool am I to travel to a foreign place alone? I have no clue where I am.* Fear, an unexpected, mighty force took me over. It crippled my thinking. The music stopped playing. I felt so small and weak…lost. *I'm alone. Puny little me, believing I could be bigger than I am. What was I thinking?* My power completely stripped from my being, I lost the ability to utter a single French word. In fact, I forgot how to speak altogether. I forgot how to listen and trust my instincts, how to be brave. I forgot how to *be*. Fear paralyzed me.

Where is Nesrine? She was supposed to meet me when I arrived. Why wasn't she here? I circled the train station. I re-read my instructions. Yes, I was to meet her there. I double-checked the times. I looked and looked and didn't even know exactly what I was searching for. *Grace,* I told myself, *don't wear your emotions on your sleeve, it could make you a target to be pick-pocketed or even kidnapped.*

I became paranoid, visualizing horrific outcomes of what could come of this situation. The joke about the movie *Taken* was a possible reality that took over my thoughts. My warrior-like spirit had abandoned me.

Grace, breathe, calm down. I took a couple deep breaths. It helped. *Hey! You have her number, call her! So simple, why didn't I think of that before?*

"Bonjour, Nesrine! C'est moi, Divine. Je suis à la gare!"

"Ah, oui, Divine. Je suis a la gare aussi! Ou es-tu?"

Hearing her voice on the other end was like seeing the light at the end of the tunnel. She was there, she said. But I still couldn't see her. I didn't know whom I was looking for. I didn't know what she looked like. I could have passed her a zillion times already.

And then I looked up and spotted my name, written on a piece of paper, held up by a lady. I squinted as if to see more clearly. Was that really *my* name? I walked a little bit closer. So it was!

Fear dissolved as I slowly approached her. She radiated pure kindness and warmth. I could feel her soul, and it was beautiful. She was beautiful. As I gazed upon her face and allowed her being to engulf my being in an embrace, I realized how familiar she looked, but I had never seen her before.

That's how I knew I was supposed to be there, exactly at that moment. I was one moment closer to my truth, because in that foreign place, with people I'd never met or seen before, I felt like I *belonged*. It felt like home. I knew somewhere in another life, in another dimension or time, I had been there before, and my soul knew this well.

Nesrine showed me the metro system, and we walked from the Metro over to her house so I would know where it was located.

As soon as we got to her home, and after walking five stories up a spiral staircase, she introduced me to her children and husband. She showed me the room I'd be staying in. It was small but perfect. It opened up to a balcony overlooking mountains in the distance. I quickly settled in and changed into something more comfortable. It felt good to get out of the clothes I'd been sitting in for the last day. As I continued organizing my things, Nesrine popped her head in.

"Allo, are you hungry? Would you like to eat with me?"

"Oh, that's very kind of you, yes, I'd love to join you!"

She had made a Niçoise salad for dinner that evening. It was delicious, paired with a glass of French wine and a baguette.

"Ahhh, so you are here alone? Do you have plans or uhhh… itinerary? Do you know where you go?"

"Um…I don't really have plans. I'm just going to go where I'm called to go. I'm sorta on an adventure."

"Ohhhh, wow! So no plans? Don't know where you are going, but you are going, oui?"

"Yes…pretty much!"

"Ahhhla vache! You are brave."

"Ha…or très stupide…" I joked.

We conversed for a little bit with her daughter who was home that weekend. Regardless of the slight language barrier, it felt like we were on the same page in conversation. I did my best to speak in French, they did their best to speak in English. I felt like I was among good friends and not strangers I had met only a couple hours earlier.

After thanking them for dinner and a time well-shared, I retired to my room and turned on my computer to connect with Keoni. *Oh, my boy, there's his sweet face!* The technology was a treat, but I wished I could reach into the screen and hold him, take in his scent, and feel him in real time. I did my best to stay present and take in every second of our interaction. We spoke for a good 20-30 minutes about how his day was going and about my trip. "Mama, I miss you. Mama I miss you," he kept saying. "Mama, kiss…" he'd say, and blow me a kiss. I had to promise him that one day I'd bring him to France (an easy wish to want to fulfill as I knew this was part of his soul's journey too).

I also took the time to check in with family and friends, like Brian, letting them know that I was safe and had made it to France!

I knew I'd probably have a good night's rest, a deep sleep, due to fatigue and lack of the adrenaline that had kept me going. Tomorrow... I was exhausted but could hardly wait... the first full day to be spent in the land of my soul's yearning!

Chapter 23

I felt refreshed the next morning. What better way to spend it than exploring the city with my own personal tour guide? Ines, Nesrine's oldest daughter, had agreed to give me a tour of the famous port city. She was brilliant and witty and had a cool artistic vibe. She would have been considered a hipster if she had been living in the States, but was actually the real deal whom hipsters in the States attempted to be like. She was more advanced and mature than most people her age I'd known. Luckily, she spoke a lot of English, which made conversations with her even more delightful. We laughed and joked about the same topics, and I could tell she appreciated depth, whether in art, music, literature, or life in general. She was the highlight of my tour of the city. I loved being able to connect with locals and being shown the gems of the city, hidden from the touristy trails. Much better than your typical "here's a famous monument and there's another famous monument, yada yada yada." I wanted to see and feel the city through the eyes of its inhabitants, the people who created life there every day.

The city was quite alluring. Marseilles was similar to San Diego, mountains in the background and ocean nearby. The weather was almost identical too, and so were the people. Marseilles was diverse, and the people were easygoing and friendly. I thought, *Wow, I could totally live here*. Ironically, I remembered how a couple people had warned me to stay away from there since it was a port city, which could result in a lot of crime. All that I saw were different walks of life and various types of life happening and being. It was colorful and vibrant and did not at all give me the vibe that it was a city full of ugliness and crime. It was, in fact, fascinating to watch the bustling town come alive as we made our way down towards the harbor.

After getting back home from the day's expedition, Nesrine excitedly once again popped her head into my room with her beaming smile.

"Allo, we are going to the beach for picnic. Will you come with us? You can see the beach here. It's beautiful. I have wine. We will have wine at the beach!"

How could anyone decline a picnic and wine on the beach to watch the sunset in the South of France? There was a Ferris wheel somewhere in the distance, and the view was just captivating. It reminded me of a classier California beach town. It was nearly 9pm, and it was still light out. I luxuriated in the moment, in the wine we slowly sipped, in the tasty French delicacies spread on the blanket before us, in the cool ocean breeze, with majestic mountains in the background, and in the amazing company. I definitely felt like I was a part of their family.

Later that evening, I decided to have a taste of the city's wild, dynamic nightlife with Ines and her friends. For sipping one drink after another, they kept themselves under control. They never got sloppy or messy like the people who indulged in the party scene back home. They stayed cool and classy till the night's end. I had a lot of admiration for this, because it was nice to see, for once, young people having fun and yet able to hold themselves together no matter how loud and crazy the atmosphere got. There was a sort of maturity behind the indulgence, a sense of control among the chaos.

Although we didn't get home until the early morning, I was able to get a good night's sleep and wake up coherent and energized. The next morning, I decided it was time to go on foot, alone, to check out other parts of Marseilles. I walked to the Metro to go down to the harbor to catch a bus that would take me up to the highest point of the city. The cathedral Notre Dame De La Garde would be my focal point for the day, standing tall on Marseilles' highest ground, observing the city below.

There were a ton of steps leading up to the cathedral that brought me to a panoramic view of the entire city. As I attempted to catch my breath, I took in the beauty before me. It was so magnificent and grand, and I wished someone was next to me to share the scene. But no, I was alone. I noticed, however, that this fact didn't sadden me. If anything, it rejuvenated me and gave me a sense of power.

I took my time walking around the grounds of the cathedral, talking to Spirit along the way. What was here that I was supposed to find? Was I to realize that the patron saint of the South of France was Mary Magdalene? I already knew that. Was I to put on my Indiana Jones hat and explore off the beaten path some more? Was I supposed to discover relics like those from my fantasies, visions, and dreams? Why did I feel it was more than that? More than simply truth about history or even my own history. No, it was about discovering truth that would help me piece things together to create my future. Maybe I was looking too hard and missing the point. Anyway, I knew I would not leave France empty-handed, or rather, empty-hearted. Sooner or later, I'd discover that which my heart and soul searched for.

That evening, after speaking to Keoni via Google hangouts and a few others from back home wanting to check in with me, I got ready to retire. I heard a knock on the door. It was Nesrine, inviting me over for a glass of wine in the kitchen. I again couldn't decline.

This was probably one of the best evenings I spent there. Nesrine, her husband Ahmed, and I, stayed up until 2:30 in the morning, conversing about history, religion, spirituality, world order, and life in general. With one glass after another, we went deeper with each topic at hand. I gained so much knowledge, was introduced to great wisdom, and created such a fun memory with two friends who had not long ago been strangers. I was filled up, simply being present in the moment, allowing myself to be, as we went back and forth in conversation.

I love how life organically connects us to individuals who help us evolve. Synchronicities remind us that there are deeper purposes to these coincidental moments. Your soul mates and people destined to help you grow one way or another are out there. Find them. Find people. Connect to people. Learn about people. And you'll never worry about a lack of adventure and thrill.

And maybe that was it. Maybe I was supposed to just be present and connect with the moment and the individuals who were part of that moment so that I could then connect with a deeper truth within myself. Maybe. It still didn't make complete sense. I wasn't sure yet what it was that I was supposed to discover. But it was getting clearer that I wasn't supposed to be like Indiana Jones, uncovering old relics. Maybe we'll save that for another story in the future, who knows.

The next day, it was raining terribly hard with winds blowing like I'd never seen or heard before. When the infamous Mistral winds of the South of France come around, it's best to stay in, so that we did. We quickly drove to the grocery store to buy things to cook. Lucky me that I was staying with a chef! Nesrine cooked and taught cooking classes for a living, so I had a private cooking class that the day. What a treat to spend a day learning how to cook a *French* dish or two, of course while sipping wine and eating French cheese!

We bought so many types of cheeses and snacked on them, along with a couple glasses of wine, while we cooked throughout the day. Nesrine taught me how to make Tarte de Pommes (an apple dessert dish) along with a pasta dish. If you ask me to make them now, I couldn't even tell you where to start. Maybe it was the wine, or maybe I didn't care to pay close attention to directions. I cared more for the experience and the hands-on moments. The results were, however, incredibly delicious. I savored every bite, wishing we had cooked more. It was one of the best rainy days I had ever spent indoors.

Later that evening, as I was deciding which city to roam next, Nesrine made me an offer.

"If you like, I come with you! I will drive us, and I can help you get to the cities you want to see."

"That would be wonderful, Nesrine! Oui – definitely oui!"

"Alors, I will make sandwich for a picnic for us tomorrow!"

"Okay, that sounds great, Nesrine. Merci… merci beaucoup."

Now I wouldn't have to get up super early and attempt to catch the train.

"It will be a treat for me, too," Nesrine said. "If you want, pay for gas, if you feel like you have to pay for something."

"That's perfect," I agreed. "An adventure for the two of us!"

Without being too indecisive about where to go, we quickly made up our minds and chose to head north to explore the city of Avignon.

The next day, morning congestion from cars on the way to work had us inching our way out of the city. The further north we drove, the less crowded the highway, but I was bummed that the clouds barely made way for blue skies.

After being on the road for a while, we realized we had missed our exit.

"Not to worry," Nesrine said. "We go to another town first, the city of Orange, same direction."

Now en route to this unexpected portion of the trip, I felt

excited. Although sometimes scary and frustrating, sudden detours prompted a thrill and an extra dose of happy anticipation.

Sure enough, I fell deeply in love with the quaint little city. I literally felt like I had been taken back in time to the Old World where, without fail, every walkway was made of cobblestone. We wandered around like the usual tourists, peeking into secret pockets of the town and exploring cute little stores strung along the empty streets. Equally nosy, we tuned in to everything going on, and took a million pictures of the most ordinary things that we found *extraordinary,* because they were different from the things that filled our worlds. We were most surprised that the city lacked busyness and the usual crowds.

As soon as we got our fill of Orange, off we went toward our initial destination. Avignon was a walled-in fortress, medieval-esque and Old World-like, similar to Orange. It underscored the advice to not judge anything from its outward appearance, because I thought it would be rather cold and desolate inside the city, but to my surprise, it was filled with life.

Once more, off we went to discover and marvel at the natural beauty this new locale offered. I had to remind myself to simply be present in each current moment. To not quickly search for something else that might be more breathtaking than the treasures laid out in front of me. To appreciate and take it all in, without looking too deeply or thinking too hard about it, because, well, I might miss the actual true beauty of it, which only existed in the present moment.

We explored the famous Les Palais des Papes (The Pope's Palace), the focal point of the city which featured magnificent gardens. Scarfing down delicious sandwiches that Nesrine had prepared for us, we sat on the grass enjoying the sunshine and indulging in the moment. We gladly took part in the art of people-watching, identifying tourists from all over the world. It was amazing to watch the scenes and delight of so many people from different countries in this quaint little garden, speaking their own languages. We were all there, harmoniously co-existing.

As the day dwindled down to the late afternoon, we decided to leave. I must have been so tired from the day's activities because I quickly fell asleep in the car and didn't wake up until we were back in Marseilles.

The next day, I decided to venture out on my own again. This time, my destination was Aix-en-Provence. I took the subway to the big metro station in order to hop on a bus which would take me to Aix. As soon as I got there, I wanted to take pictures of the cute little alleyways and shops (there were so many). But again, I had to remind myself to slow down and put my camera away in order to capture still shots of the moment with my heart instead. People were super friendly; they acknowledged me, saying hello as I passed by. I think it would be safe to call this city a Paris of the South of France. The energy and vibe felt like Paris but a little more subdued, a little more Old World, and not as busy. Another city to fall in love with.

In the midst of gallivanting from one end of Aix to another, I sat myself down for lunch on the terrace of a small cafe and observed the bustling city and passersby in my view. I journaled a bit and became true to the moment. I respected it by slowing down, pausing. And then I reflected on my life. There I was, at a cafe in Provence, enjoying a glass of wine, people-watching and admiring how truly beautiful life could be when one paused. It was crazy to remember how different my life had been not that long ago. I had been so anxious, preparing myself for one of the hardest transitions of my life. I would never have thought that a year later I'd be doing well on my own, fulfilling my dream of visiting the South of France. So much had changed; the comparison was shocking. I'd been a person filled with fear and doubts, but now I'd become free and filled with peace.

Before I left the city where Ines attended university, I waited until late afternoon for her to meet me for a drink. As we dove into conversation one last time, we toasted to the adventures of life and then said our goodbyes. I would not see her again for the remainder of my trip, as I planned to head to Paris in the next couple of days. As we parted ways, my spirit shined a little brighter, as I deposited one more token of love and gratitude for moments shared with Ines. I am certain I will see her again a handful more times in this lifetime.

After debating over which city to travel to next, I decided on the Languedoc Roussillon region and the small city of Nimes. Nimes was one of the few Roman cities in the South of France that was filled with Romanesque architecture and monuments, including its own colosseum that resembled the famous Colosseum in Rome.

Nesrine agreed to accompany me again. She drove, I paid for gas, and we shared stories along the way. Though a tad gloomy and rainy, it was an enchanting drive. If anything, the rain and clouds added to the mystifying energy.

Then, oddly, I got teary-eyed and started to cry. I couldn't tell you why. There was something about the energy of the place we were driving through. Chills ran up and down my body, and sadness engulfed me.

"Divine? Are you okay?" Nesrine asked as soon as she realized I was in tears.

"Where are we, Nesrine?"

"Ahhh, we are now in the Languedoc Rousillon region. Are you okay? Why you are crying?"

"I don't know. I'm not sure why I'm crying. I feel the energy here is strong. There's something special about this place."

In an instant I knew my soul had been there before, perhaps in a past life. What a beautiful feeling to have my soul secretly remember a sacred place that was part of its history and physically react to it. I closed my eyes and made peace with it. Whatever hurt and whatever wound was present, I thought, *Let it be healed and let it have peace.* I may not know the complete details of that life or lives once lived there, but I did know that whatever karmic contract it created and had attached to my soul, was now complete and no longer. *Let all be forgiven and set free. Let my soul move forward.* I had to release that part of my spirit free so it could finally grow. As I finished my meditation, clearing energy and sending it peace, forgiveness, and love, I immediately felt lighter. I had finally made peace with that part of my soul.

Arriving in Nimes, the clouds rolled in some more, and the sky darkened in color. We continued our adventure on foot anyway. Exploring the city of Nimes was quite a delight, even with the rain pouring down. People and things got wet and yet didn't seem to care or become too bothered by it. Locals were just as kind and warm as people I'd met when the sun had been high in the sky and blue skies had stretched from one end of the atmosphere to the other. As we finished touring the famous colosseum, shops, some ruins and a watch tower, we decided to call it a day. It was a short trip, maybe because of the rain (we weren't able to explore on foot as much as we wanted), but nonetheless, I'd needed to touch base with that region before I left the South.

Before we headed out, Nesrine encouraged me to taste France's famous alcoholic beverage, Pastis. Definitely a drink meant to be slowly sipped. It was strong and tasted like licorice, which may or may not be bad depending on your preference. For me, though, I think I'll pass on Pastis next time around.

Our drive back home was spent sharing deeper parts of our souls. We were like old friends sharing in conversation and identifying with one another's stories. The small language barrier was no hindrance to understanding each other. And maybe it was because we were learning about one another on a more meaningful level than on previous days.

When you become completely present with others, you can feel their souls, see them for who they are. She was a beautiful soul whom I felt was on a journey to find herself, hoping for purpose and thrills in life again, seeking peace and healing of past wounds. Her story was similar to mine, and maybe that was why we were able to connect and understand one another.

Our willingness to be honestly present with each other during my trip was a poignant gift for both of us. We never know when we, ourselves, are acting as angels for others, to be a refuge, an inspiration, a new way of looking at life that becomes a beam of hope. We gave one another solace for sensitive things shared, and gratitude for the beautiful way we served one another's needs in our interaction. In the end, it's a give and take, a sharing, a coming together to support one another's highest and greatest good. She did for me as I did for her. It was quite the perfect and beautiful karmic exchange between souls.

As I headed to bed that night, I thought of how much we really are all alike. We have the same fears and insecurities. We have the same desires, hopes, and dreams that root from similar places. But we complicate life. We build walls against one another and create wars. We hurt one another instead of love one another. We compete and become jealous. We judge instead of accept. Why is it so difficult to allow ourselves to love, be loved, and BE Love in its entirety? To understand one another and give each other the freedom to be? To understand and accept why and when people come and go or moments occur and end. To simply understand that each of these changeable pieces are part of a bigger plan created by ourselves to help one another grow as souls. There is never an end; as I have seen each and every one of you before in lifetimes past, I shall see each and every one of you again in lifetimes after. I have loved you all, and you have loved me. And outside of this human body, we know this. It really is that simple, is it not?

After much introspection the previous night, I decided I'd spend my last full day in the South of France near the coast, in the small port town of Cassis. It was known as the mini St. Tropez, but without the glitz, glamour, and bourgeois style of the other French Riviera beach cities. Quaint and provincial, the city boasted farmhouses and vineyards galore. Nesrine and I visited a couple vineyards on the way there and back. We explored the beautiful, charming town, taking a look at what merchants had to offer at an outside market before heading down to the water. And then we decided to take a boat tour of the calanques. As we marveled at river's carved inlets, I made friends with the boat captain and opted for a chance to drive the boat for a short time. It was definitely a good, relaxing last day in the South of France, lighter in energy than the day before and the perfect way to spend my last few hours. Nesrine and I toasted our wine glasses to the sea and to life and the many adventures our souls would continue to embark on.

That evening before bed, I wanted to sit in meditation and send gratitude to the Angels, to the Ascended Masters, and to God for giving me such a wonderful experience in the South of France. As I sat down, though, I knew it was more than just a meditation set on the intention of gratitude. I knew I had some work to do. Going back to the way I'd felt as we'd entered the Languedoc Roussillon region, I knew I needed to do some letting go from this present life as well. Karmic contracts were being completed and coming full circle. I thought, *What's there to let go of?* I thought I'd forgiven, made peace, and let go of the one thing that had recently caused me deep pain: my divorce. But as I realized I was still hurting from that, I asked for guidance.

In my mind and heart, I had let go of Paul; I had set him free, forgiven him for any hurt he had caused me in the past, and had allowed healing. So who was I still angry with? I then realized who it was: myself.

Although my intention for our divorce had been to live healthier, happier, and more fulfilling lives, I had gotten stuck in feeling guilty for hurting him, for not being a *good wife,* for feeling like I had abandoned him in order to serve myself, and for leaving the one man I had loved in the last handful of years. I needed to free myself from guilt, from blame, from hurt. As much as I believed that Paul deserved happiness, I deserved it too, and I needed to believe that. How had I failed to love myself in this regard? How could I have freed all the other prisoners from my fears and insecurities but not myself?

I called in the Angels, Source, Spirit, God, and the Ascended Masters, hoping they'd hear my plea for help, but I knew this battle was in my own hands. It was up to me to free myself. I looked at the guilt and the hurt I still held in my heart, and I asked: How had it served me? It had protected me from venturing off into that which I hadn't been ready for; which, if I had allowed to come into my life when I wasn't ready, would have failed. I needed to let go, to set myself free from that which had been present even before Paul had come into my life.

I hadn't loved myself then because I hadn't known how to. I had been told several times of the beautiful life I would live, and I had been certain those predictions were correct, so I'd waited for life to unravel itself instead of creating my own flow. Up until a year ago, I'd sat and waited for the Universe to create magic *for* me. It had now and then, almost like reminders from Source that I was capable of controlling my own fate- from buying a home at 21 to opening up a business to manifesting the France trip, to name a few. And while my own desires were catalysts and my efforts the fuel that turned wishes into achievements, I suffered from a form of amnesia - forgetting that I need not wait for life to create a fate for me. Faith in my foretold destiny to be great, to become my true self, my own God Self, couldn't be sustained. I hadn't fully integrated the deep knowing that it was up to me to get there by stepping into my power.

My entire life I had struggled with identity. I'd carried several names before I turned 18. My grandfather's name, my dad's, going back and forth over whether to use Divine, my first name, or Grace, my middle name. There were times when I aspired to be Divine: powerful, knowing, brave, and God-like. And other times when I'd needed to allow myself Grace and simply honor my humanity. I'd always received messages from Spirit, telling me that my answers were found in my name. It'd never dawned on me, what that meant on so many levels. I realized, I am Divine Grace. I am God, here in the physical plane, having a human experience, needing grace and the gentle hand of forgiveness every so often.

As are we all. If we identify with our own God Self and honor It, we naturally abandon our fears and doubts and are able to create an abundance of happiness, love, and peace. But it's not that easy. Because we are also humans who experience human emotions that sometime force us to retreat back into our caves.

However, sitting in the guest room in France, I was no longer afraid. I needed to trust in my faith – all the time. The only thing left to do as I stepped into my own God Self was to love myself fully by understanding my pain and forgiving myself, thus liberating my spirit. I needed to forgive myself for: holding myself back, putting myself in hurtful situations, accepting blame that wasn't mine, and for not supporting and loving my Self the way I had wanted others to.

I was at a loss as to what emotions I should entertain. It was a mixture of sadness, peace, joy, and love. It's incredible how much a person or a moment can truly affect your evolution. And it seems that the most painful of goodbyes are the ones that touch us the deepest, changing forevermore the direction of our paths.

Paul and I are undeniably one pair of each other's soul mates. The connection we shared had its ever so beautiful moments as well as its ugly and painful ones. But that's life, and through these experiences, we evolve as souls, thus helping one another ascend. When we create our soul contracts with our soul mates before we enter lifetimes, we agree to help one another with whatever life lessons we need to learn, in order to ascend and become one with the Universe. Often we forget to do them in the name of Love. And that is why the lesson of forgiveness is so important—when spiritual school is harsh, leaving us feeling attacked or hurt. We must put effort into looking at experiences as a whole and from a bigger perspective and to understand that we're all here just doing the same thing: having a human experience, checking off lessons, and learning Love on all its levels.

We must learn to forgive people for being themselves. Somewhere, sometime ago, they too, were hurt or lacked love, and a void was left, which in turn allowed them to do such hurt unto you. But perhaps this is the lesson we needed to learn with them in this lifetime.

Our greatest teachers sometimes are the ones who challenge us to our very cores, who test us and see if we are able to stand our ground with grace, regardless of what is thrown at us. Often we learn and grow the most when pushed down to rock bottom or into a corner. It is up to us to remember who we are (Gods) and avoid falling into fear and self-doubt. There is no part of my soul (or anyone else's) that is not that which is Love, and which is God. I know this, and I trust it. Unveiling my true identity that night allowed me to step into my power.

The next morning, I devoured the usual, delicious breakfast that Nesrine had prepared before I left for my train ride up to Paris. The morning was filled with so much emotion. These people had once been strangers. Only eight days later, they had become family, and I didn't want to leave. I didn't want to miss them. They had become a part of me, a part of my story.

As we embraced as I thanked them over and over for their hospitality and friendship. "Thank you so much for everything. I will never forget this and will be back. You have all left a huge imprint on my heart."

"Oh Divine, I am going to miss you. You are different, and there will be no one else like you to come stay here; I know this. Come see us again. Bring your son with you!"

"I definitely will. I will always think of you all. Don't be strangers! I love you all."

"Bon voyage, Divine. Je t'aime aussi. I will miss you," bid Nesrine as I headed out with my luggage in hand.

Ahmed took me to the train station. I gave him a final hug, a final thank you, and a see you again, because I knew I would someday. I boarded my train, already missing my new family. In a few hours… Paris!

Chapter 24

After a few hours of writing on the train and appreciating the mesmerizing views of the countryside, I arrived in Paris. In two days I'd return home, back to Keoni.

Having half a day left, I explored half of the city. It was as breathtaking and magical as I'd thought it would be. It was a rainy day in Paris, and I walked around the city under my new umbrella. It was as romantic, as I had hoped. I had dinner near the hotel that night. Nothing too fancy, just to fill myself up so I'd have energy the next morning to check out the rest of the city. Taking the Metro as I made my way back to the hotel, I felt more alone than I had in Marseilles. But just like when I stood at Notre Dame De La Garde, being alone didn't sadden me as it would have before; I felt powerful. In fact, I was super excited to start the next day extra early. There was freedom in being alone – I could follow any schedule I chose.

I was happy to see blue in the sky and the sun shining when I stepped out the next morning. Every famous monument you could think of I walked to and marveled at, taking pictures galore with my camera and with my heart, absorbing energy and sharing conversations with anyone willing. I took time to lie in the grass looking up at the Eiffel Tower and to be completely and utterly present in the moment. I couldn't believe I was finally there.

Although every cool landmark in Paris was on my to-see list, I reminded myself to slow down here and there in order to fully take everything in. I stopped and took breaks at gardens and parks, listened to a live band, and allowed myself to put my feet up and observe the life and people in my current scene. I explored the famous bookstore, Shakespeare and Company, and was randomly invited to join a group that shared thoughts in conversation about books and the arts. Those attending passed around sandwiches and invited me to help myself to one. I felt good and brave injecting myself into a group filled with strangers, openly sharing enlightening conversations. I simply felt happy.

I stopped by Pont Neuf and watched the passersby. I strolled into a cafe to sit and enjoy a cup of coffee while I observed life happening around me. I'd told Brian I'd take a pause on the bridge for him. I missed him and wished he was there with me. *But he's not, so stop wishing he was.* I needed to stay present with what was in front of me, and unfortunately, he wasn't. Throughout the duration of my trip, we had Facetimed every now and then. He'd gotten up early and talked to me while still in bed, as I'd sat on my bed before rushing out for a late dinner. I'd checked in with him and shared about my day and vice versa. *But it's not going to happen. I can tell, he's colder... He's leaving me! Getting out of the relationship, even though it's just a friendship.* And that awareness cut through the haze that had obscured my true feelings. *Oh my God. I love him. More than as a friend... Why didn't I tell him? If only I'd spoken up all those times when he'd hinted at feelings for me... I should have spoken my truth and not cared about getting rejected or heartache or whether he felt the same way about me. Ha! I was afraid of losing my friend, and I've lost him anyway. Maybe it didn't have to be like this, but I know it's too late... I'm going to miss him so much.*

As the sun set, I got off the ferry taxi and decided to walk along the Seine. Being in the present moment was where living happened. There was no point dwelling or focusing anywhere else. I breathed deeply and happiness was restored. Look where I was! Look indeed, everyone I walked past were couples. Canoodling, embracing, or making out while walking along the Seine at sunset. I was the only person walking by themselves. Of course I was. This was a famous river in the most romantic city in the world at sunset!

It didn't matter. I didn't feel sad or jealous or nostalgic for anything I'd had in the past. No. I felt at peace. In my meditation last night I'd done the inner work of setting myself free, finally unveiling my true self, and stepping into that power. I could feel that energy seeping in. I was genuinely and deeply happy. I had discovered my truth and the kind of Love I had been searching for the last 28 years. It was a Love only found deeply within oneself, going hand-in-hand with one's true identity: Self Love.

The once bottomless pit of a void within me was filling up. This was ultimate freedom, to be liberated from the confines of doubts, insecurities, and fears. I didn't need anyone else to fulfill that happiness for me, because I had discovered it within. I felt invincible and utterly happy. Yeah, I knew this wasn't the end of the trail. Maintaining this state of joy would require work and continuous reminding of one's true self. Life makes pretty powerful attempts to get us to forget who we are.

I looked at the boats dreamily floating down the Seine. Lovers sat close to each other, enjoying the close of the day. *I'm ready for you, true love.* I knew that coming across a love that would mirror what I now bestowed on myself was only a matter of time. I needn't worry or be impatient about its arrival. Divine timing is when the Universe happens to bring you that which you need for your present moment, never too early, never delayed, always in time and on time. *Paris, you did not disappoint.*

Returning home from France, I felt energized and empowered.

"Keoni!" I knelt down and he rushed into my arms.

"Mama!"

I held him in a tight embrace for as long as I could. I didn't want to let go and neither did he.

"I missed you so much, Mama!"

"Me, too! I missed YOU so much!"

Seeing him in the physical, feeling his touch, hearing his voice as he kept telling me how much he had missed me and how much he loved me...ahhhh! This was love in its ever so perfect way. To be present with such a soul mate of mine and share in this energy of gigantic love, this was heaven and such the welcome home that I'd needed. I trust in my son's love for me, knowing for certain that nothing and no one outside of us will ever be able to change it.

I allowed the energy around me to unfold on its own. I continued to internally work on myself. I spent most of my free time in meditation, manifesting my ideal life and releasing what I needed to let go of. With Brian out of my world, I felt the Universe was helping to clear a path so I could create space to bring in the ideal relationship. Of course I was curious about the man I was supposed to meet after I got back from France.

I envisioned a healthy relationship based on friendship (similar to the standard set with Brian—he banter, the jokes, support, encouragement, admiration and respect), but injected with romance, passion, and thrill. A connection built of honesty, trust, and acceptance—so we'd feel safe being real with each other, able to call each other out when necessary.

I wanted someone who would honor my freedom and independence. And my soul was ready to co-create with a life partner in a way that would grow, ground, and empower us. Couples always act as mirrors for each other, and it helps when both people know it!

Something especially important on my thorough list (always good to be specific when setting your intentions!), was to be with someone who Keoni could grow to love, who would love Keoni – a partner who would deeply enjoy being a step-parent. Not someone to replace Paul, no. A parent in a child's life can never be replaced, especially if they are very present. I wasn't looking for a new father for him. I was seeking a man who'd be a positive male role model for my son.

I wrote these attributes on note cards. I meditated on them and created a strong vision filled with all those details. This was part of me stepping into my power, realizing my God self and co-creating with the Universe that which I desired and intended to manifest.

Fast forward to a couple months later. My birthday was coming up, and my friends and I were going out on the town to celebrate. My friend, Ariel, told me to look up places on Yelp to decide where to go. Nothing appealed to me except for one whiskey bar in the area, *Seven Grand*. I had been seeing the number seven a lot recently, so maybe that was why it called to me. However, within the next couple days, my friends decided they wanted to go to a different bar, in the opposite direction from where I wanted to go. Although excited to check out the other bar, I still had Seven Grand on my mind. As we walked out of the house, something stopped me, and right then and there I knew I needed to go to Seven Grand that night.

"Guys, I'm going to make the executive decision to change our plans. Let's head down to the bar I first mentioned. I don't know why, but I need to be there tonight. You know I can't ignore a nudge from the Universe when something's calling me," I said. And it was, in fact, *my* birthday that we were celebrating after all, so I figured I should be the one to decide where I wanted to celebrate it.

When we got to the area where the bars were, my friends made a left instead of a right, and we ended up going into another bar instead. Shocked, my friend Odessa realized she had forgotten her driver's license and didn't have any ID to show the bouncers at the door. We worked some magic, though, and somehow finagled the bouncers into allowing her through the doors. As we made our way in, my friends quickly headed for the bar to grab me my first birthday drink of the night. I was stoked that we'd gotten Odessa in; however, I was anxious to sip my way to the bottom of my drink so that we could quickly leave for Seven Grand.

As we walked to Seven Grand, I remembered that Odessa would have to haggle her way through the doors again. It had surely been pure luck the last time the bouncers let her in; I hoped and wished with everything I had that a repeat event was in her future. Our ladylike sweet talk and her charm inspired them to allow Odessa to enter. My friends wanted to explore the place, but for some reason, I was attracted to the back of the bar. It was a secluded room where a band played, people lounged and danced, and plenty of whiskey went around. It was my kind of bar. Nothing too fancy or glamorous, but cool in its simplicity.

My friends ordered their drinks and proceeded to the dance floor. I stood at the bar still deciding on a drink. Ariel came up to me to try to take a selfie of us with her phone. I just wanted my glass of whiskey and started feeling a little annoyed. She kept having to re-take the picture. Exasperated, I grabbed her phone, and handed it to the first guy I saw.

"Hey, can you please take a picture of us?" I asked.

"Sure," he said, and quickly clicked a successful one.

"Thanks," I said, handing Ariel's phone to her.

Glad it was time to sip on my whiskey, I walked over to the dance floor to listen to the band playing. I was in my own little world, enjoying the moment, and happened to glance up. (Or maybe I felt energy coming my way.) The guy who had taken the photo was casually approaching me. *Definitely has a cool vibe... and nice smile.* I took in his dark brown eyes and short dark hair. *Handsome.* I saw how lean and fit he was. *He must work out. Looks like someone safe to talk to.*

"I'm not sure if this band has sung a single word of English this whole time," he said.

I listened consciously, and he was right. It sounded like they were just mumbling or yelling. I laughed because it was actually funny and replied back with something either stupid or witty, because from there, we continued to laugh and banter back and forth.

Going with the flow of the night, I had listened to the Universe's gentle nudge to open up and share, and here I stood in the middle of the dance floor with a stranger who was funny and interesting enough to dive into conversation with. I don't even remember what we talked and joked about, but he was charming, handsome, smart, and incredibly funny. He had my attention for sure, and no, it wasn't the whiskey, it was him. It was his brain, his dry, sarcastic wit, his humor, and his charm. We talked for only 20 minutes, but that was all it took to pique my curiosity. Who was he?! Unfortunately, he and his friend needed to leave earlier than expected. I was bummed.

"Good talk. See ya later," I said.

He leaned over to me. "Hey, what's your P.O Box number? I want to send you a postcard."

I thought, *Okay, I'll banter back*. "Dude, really? A postcard would take way too long to get to me."

I could tell by the disappointment on his face that he had just felt rejected.

"Oh, alright, well it was nice talking to you then..." he said.

I laughed at the fact that he seemed to be giving up so easily and felt bad for making him feel like I turned down an invite to continue creating a connection. "Or wait, hold on, maybe there's something else we can do? What about email?" I said. "Hmm... no, email would take too long as well." I held my phone up and examined it with a pretend puzzled look. "What about this?"

"Ohhhhhh yeahhhh, that could work..."

I was getting a little frustrated that he still wouldn't ask for my number. I knew he wanted it, because, well, he hadn't left and continued to entertain my comebacks. I cut to the chase and said, "You know, you *could* just ask for my number and actually call me one of these days or something. You know, something like that…"

"Yeah, you know, I think that could work! I think I like that idea…"

"Alright, well, I think I'm okay with that too."

We exchanged numbers. His name was Steve, and I told him my name was Divine Grace. I knew he'd look me up on social media, and I wanted to make sure he'd find me, so I gave him both my first and middle name—to give him a head start. Synchronized with Steve leaving the scene, my friend Ariel needed to call it a night as well, and surprisingly, I was okay with that. I felt like whatever I'd needed to see or experience that night had happened. We returned to my house, and my friends Odessa and Valerie stayed over until early the next morning. To my surprise, Steve had texted me by the time they left. Turns out, based on the number he had texted me from, he was from New Jersey. I didn't recall hearing an accent, though.

We texted back and forth for a good 10 days. Enjoying the range of topics, we decided to hang out for happy hour or dinner. I suggested a wine bar nearby. However, when I got home from work that day, I had a message typed out and ready to send to Steve, telling him that I wasn't going to make it. I wasn't feeling 100% and didn't feel like socializing, let alone with someone I barely knew. I thought, *We're just hanging out anyway, no harm there. We can hang out some other time. It's not like a date or anything.* My friend, Ariel, though, strongly advised not sending the text and to go anyway, so off I went.

I got there a little early, so I grabbed us a table. As he walked in, he recognized me right away. Immediately, we were talking like old friends, easily and comfortably. My friends and I frequented the wine bar, so I knew what was good to snack and sip. I asked for garlic fries along with more garlic aioli and bread.

"With an order like that, I hope you like each other a lot," she said, walking off.

It didn't faze me. I honestly looked at it like we were hanging out like friends, nothing romantic, although I was definitely attracted to him. I was a fan of his energy and his being. I *loved* conversing with this guy. And before long, our waitress had to tell us that her shift had ended and someone else would be taking over. I looked at the time. Three hours had gone by, yet it only felt like maybe 30 minutes.

Wow, who was this guy?! Why was it so easy to be with him? I thought, *I'm really, really enjoying my time right now; I don't want it to end.*

As we started to leave the restaurant, I casually invited him over to my place to talk some more, not thinking of anything beyond that. On my way home, I made a call to Ariel.

"Ariel, I wanted to let you know I'm going back to my apartment with Steve."

"What? Really? Way to go, Grace. I never expected *that*!" she said.

"No, it's not like that. I really just want to keep talking to him. I'm enjoying my time with him. And so I wanted to tell you, 'thank you,' for encouraging me to go out tonight. I'm *really* enjoying myself."

When we arrived at my place, I changed out of my work clothes and got comfortable. Steve and I moved from the living room to the balcony to enjoy the summer evening. I was taken aback by how much depth and range we had in our conversation that evening. One minute we were making immature, down-to-earth jokes and the next we were talking about life philosophies, politics, spirituality, and our most intimate personal stories. Somewhere in the middle of our time talking, I felt sparks. This was not going to be just a friendship. I felt safe and free with him. I wanted to learn more about him, learn who he was, what made him laugh, smile, feel alive, what made him *him*. I had butterflies in my stomach as he unconsciously placed his hand on my leg while we were speaking. *Who are you, and why did it take you so long to get here*? I knew who he was. Of course I did...

And just like that, we looked at the time and saw it was 3:30am. We had literally talked for 10 hours straight. It turned out that he had a flight to catch later that morning at 10:30 and still needed to pack. I, on the other hand, needed to get up super early and leave the house by 7:30 in the morning.

"We'll get together soon," he said.

"Definitely," I agreed, smiling.

He leaned over and kissed me. It was soft and intimate, and I knew the potential for passion was strong. My heart raced and my stomach lurched. I was excited and nervous at the same time. *How will this unfold?* I could barely get to sleep for the few hours that remained until I had to get ready for work.

Steve and I didn't see each other for another two weeks due to our schedules. After that, we were pretty much inseparable. Our first few dates were 8-10 hours long, filled with lengthy, robust conversations and life stories. We learned a lot about each other. By the end of our second date, I felt like I had known him for years.

Soon enough, we became an official couple, and our family and friends were stoked for us. Three months into our relationship, we had pretty much moved in together. At four months, we booked flights to Europe, and few months later, we took our first international trip together to Italy and France. And then 11 months later, our home caught on fire.

That night, we slept in a hotel room, and at two o'clock in the morning, we were laughing about the disastrous day. We were always finding the lightness in situations, honing in on the beauty in things, no matter how heavy or negative a situation seemed to be. We kept one another optimistic and hopeful at all times. Still joking about how terrible our day had been, Steve got up and returned to bed with a ring.

"I love that as we sit here in this hotel room, because our home caught on fire, we're laughing still and finding light in all of it. In spite of everything that's happened today, we're making jokes and looking forward with so much optimism and faith. Most people would be so stressed out and fighting with each other right now. But with us, we're sitting here laughing about it. There's no one else I'd rather be going through this with, than with you. And I know that for anything else I have to go through, I'd want to go through it with you at my side. I can't stand going any longer without officially knowing that you're going to be my wife and that I'll spend the rest of my life with you. Grace, will you marry me?"

And just like that, we were engaged. Less than a year later, I became his wife. And I know what you must be thinking:

"That was way too fast."

"You didn't give yourself enough time to heal or maybe do more work on your own."

"You weren't on your own long enough."

"How do you know he's the one? You didn't explore enough."

"So you're living the life you've always dreamed of living because you got married again, because of a guy?"

Yada, yada, yada...

Let's talk basic magic and truth here.

Time is but an illusion, whether it takes too long or not long enough. We can make things happen in a short moment's time or in a century's time; it's up to us to define the length of time it takes for us to create. When it comes to manifestation and creation, most of us aren't able to do it quickly because, frankly, it takes a while for most people to align themselves to the same vibration of that which they are attempting to manifest. *If* we held laser-like focus on it, it would instantly be realized in our reality. But apparently, that's a myth, an impossible task, and/or magic (which supposedly isn't real), to any normal human being, that is.

My relationship with Steve mirrors the relationship I have with myself. I have total respect and confidence in him. I trust him and know he has my best interests in mind. I never doubt him (only when he believes he can cook a better Thanksgiving turkey than I can). I honor and greatly admire him for who he is. I am so in love with him, not the idea or potential of him, but all of *him*.

And I'm in love with our relationship. We flirt, schedule dates, and put in effort to woo and win each other every single day. I'm not talking about showering one another with fancy gifts or expensive outings. We're fully present when together—being real and down to earth, which includes laughing at ourselves, each other, and silly things all the time.

Yeah, you might be thinking that we're still in the "honeymoon phase." Truth be told, that phase lasted a couple of months, if that. But we were committed to mastering the art of recreating that exhilarating "honeymoon phase." And that gets juxtaposed next to being super open and honest (like maybe a bit too much sometimes). We have our fair share of disagreements, but we never *fight*. Where the heck is one's heart in that? And if there's no heart, then how can we call this a relationship or even love? I don't ever attack him or feel I need to prove myself to him. We're never in *combat* with one another, because we're more interested in understanding the other versus our egos trying to win or be right. It's good to have differences in opinions, to be your own person, and not always in sync, but for goodness sake, be respectful and kind about it. It's ridiculously easy for people to forget to be kind in their relationships, forget to simply communicate and take time to appreciate the other, laugh together at the stupid and frustrating things in life.

And no, this doesn't mean our relationship is boring. It's thrilling and passionate on so many different levels! When you feel safe and accepted and can reveal your true self to your partner, then feeling uninhibited is one more gift.

Honestly, the reason we're able to continuously maintain

a healthy and passion-filled relationship is because we continue to do the work on ourselves. We can't have healthy relationships with others if we don't strive to have a healthy relationship with ourselves first.

Steve is, without a doubt, the person I'm meant to spend the rest of my life with. He knew that Keoni was my world, and accepted the stipulation that a good relationship with my son, was essential. I am forever grateful that he is evolved enough to understand and support that. Respecting the relationship Keoni has with his dad, Steve was mindful to not put pressure on my son to force a relationship. Through his fun, easy-going personality and genuine interest in others, Steve easily and naturally became a friend and mentor to Keoni. And Keoni, trusting and feeling safe with him, has become Steve's biggest fan, next to me and my in-laws. Steve has treated Keoni as if he were his own, without crossing any lines. In this way, we do our part to bring peace to our complicated family situation.

I'm not saying I met someone cool, got married again, and boom, I got my happily ever after. No. I had found happiness and bliss before he came into my life, remember? Don't forget about the part where I worked on myself! It took me years. I broke down several times, rode the roller coaster up, and then rode it down screaming my head off, wishing I hadn't been on that ride at all. I kissed rock bottom a handful more times than I wanted. But through it all, I did the *work*. Everything I had ever wanted in a partner and relationship, I manifested because I created the space for it in my life, I believed it was mine to have, and I worked to make myself receptive to its arrival. The more I made peace with myself, the more I realized and accepted who I truly am: this mighty creator who is able to create anything she wants at any given point.

And you are, too.

Chapter 25

It took 29 years to figure out, to a good extent, how to truly love myself. Two years later, I am still practicing how to maintain this. There are days when I feel the strike to an emotional chord or two, and I immediately sit in meditation or take a brief time-out from the world to examine what is disturbing my peace. It may take days or even weeks to fully process something. But this is the one thing I emphasize with clients whom I empower to love and learn about themselves: you have to be willing to *always* do the work. We are never done.

Maybe it's laziness or discomfort or fear that gets in our way. If we accept responsibility for accessing our power, we'll need to act on it. We fear it will be too much of a task for us to uphold. But to *not* do this is to play the victim, and self-pity only leads to self-destruction. Sustaining effort to work on ourselves is key to helping us stay aligned and accountable to our truths and helps us follow through with our purpose. It is not always easy, but we must stay in contact with our inner selves and do the work. I wasn't always ready for more challenges, but the Universe's flow is non-stop. One can't refuse to move and still expect to be perfectly in-sync with it.

The deeper I go into my spirituality, the more I realize that the journey to mastery is the journey to mastering oneself. And through each and every one of my experiences, I had to learn what that meant. I had to take control of my life and shift the energy to flow in the way I intended it to go, to consciously create, consciously direct, and consciously move my life based on my own intentions and my own will. When will we realize that we ourselves are the true masters of our fates? We are Gods. When will we stop pretending that we're not? By stepping into our power and honoring our true nature as creators, the possibilities are endless.

And the sooner we make connecting with our spiritual heart a priority, a constant practice in our daily lives, the sooner it becomes second nature, something we don't have to think too hard about. Things, events, and people start to show up instantly. You'll experience magic, and life as you know it will never be the same after that, in a good way. You'll naturally tune-in to others around you and the world as a whole. Nothing will feel too scary or too big to conquer. Some things may frighten you now and then, but fear will no longer paralyze you, nor will it hold you back.

When we constantly connect with our innermost selves, it becomes effortless to recognize reminders of our truths, validation that we are on the right path, and clues from the Universe and from Spirit as to what path to take, what to create, and how to create. These reminders may be subtle or in disguise as events or particular people who enter our lives. I'll always be grateful for the people who have shown up in my life to help remind me of my truth, to help move me along in the right direction, and ultimately, to help me learn Love on many different levels.

These people who help us? Soul mates. Soul mates are not always romantic. They are our brothers, sisters, parents, children, family, friends, teachers, partners, neighbors, the people that come into our lives for a mere season, and those who stay their whole lives...and yes, even those who cross our paths whom we are not our absolute fans of, and vice versa, they are our soul mates, too. All enter our lives based on a soul contract, to help us learn lessons in order to balance our karma and ascend.

So let's try to understand and forgive them for how they've hurt us, and forgive ourselves for how we've hurt them. Human beings don't process correctly or enough, and tend to project fears and insecurities from the past onto present and future interactions—often with those they love the most. And often, people aren't aware of how they've hurt us (or prefer to keep that knowledge out of their consciousness).

I might never get an apology from people who have hurt me in my life, but I would need to do without one if I wanted to move forward and set myself free. In their minds, they have done nothing wrong. However, certain experiences and interactions wounded me. And I needed to understand why they were the way they were, and focus on sending that hurt part of myself, compassion and love, without receiving an apology on their end. Affirming our wounded parts helps us to forgive; self-love strengthens the parts of ourselves that feel weak. Forgiveness is more for YOU than for the other person. Forgive and let go because you love yourself enough to give yourself peace and healing.

In addition to soul mates who help us evolve through painful experiences, so, too, are there soul mates who enter our lives to remind us of our true selves and help us balance out our karma through a more *positive* and *enjoyable* experience. And how joyful do we feel when we meet them! Keoni and Steve, of course, dear friends in the States and France, mentors, so many others. Which leads us to another essential topic.

Love radiates in multiple layers. And while I had a fairly firm grasp on loving myself, guess what! The second major love lesson (seldom talked about), demanded its due: how to receive love from others.

One would think the task of receiving love is a simple and easy one. But when you've been stubbornly independent your entire life, when you've constructed walls to barricade your heart from hurt, it becomes immensely difficult. Life's funny; sometimes it is easier to think of ourselves as not good enough than to face ourselves and uncover the truth that we are more than good enough - more lovable and powerful than we ever thought possible. And it may take years to figure it out.

Are our lives predestined, written out before we get here, cursed, or maybe even blessed by the way our planets and stars align at our birth? Or do we ultimately have free will to choose how our stories are written out and possess the power to stir the sands of time and fate leading them to flow in a way that fulfills our desires?

I think maybe it's both. Maybe we have a destiny - always a good one - and it is up to us to get to it. Maybe there are certain markers in time when the Universe pauses other realities (that we may not be fans of), and opens up *possibility*, thereby allowing our free-will to cancel, alter, create, or even enhance what's been laid before us. And maybe it does this to give us a chance, an opportunity, to go forth and create like the mighty creators we are, if we so choose. Maybe one day we'll learn the answer.

Even if everything I've shared was fabricated in my mind (my dreams, my experiences, the messages and the loving nudges from Spirit), I was still able to create a life of joy and peace and limitless possibilities through *faith*. If anything, what this taught me was to hold on to faith, no matter what. To believe in something bigger than you, bigger than life. And to have complete and utter trust in it. I don't care what you call it, God, Universe, Allah, Buddha, Energy, Source, Universe, Spirit, etc. I don't even care if you believe in any of that. I don't care if you're religious, spiritual, or an atheist. You just need to believe in something, something that embodies the magnificence of life that elevates you to a plane greater than life itself. That belief is fundamental. Whether it's an ambush of hugs from your admiring child, a gentle hand squeeze from a spouse covertly signaling a reminder of their love, the unconditional wagging of your dog's tail when you come home, or any other of life's beautiful, small, nameless moments, or on a more serious note, your strength to conquer fear and defy the odds, to create magic when no one else believes in it, when nobody else believes in you. Believe in something purely good. Hold on to faith firmly, with all of your being. Because in the end, it really just comes down to faith. How much faith you have to make something happen, to change your life for the better.

In my journey thus far, through my faith, I became an alchemist performing the greatest transmutation of all time. I experienced and performed magic, because I believed in it so much and did the work that manifested it. I transformed my whole world from being in a state of fear, to state of being in Love.

In the middle of watching my life beautifully unfold, I had the recurring dream where I was being chased by *something* on my grandmother's street, except this time, I was no longer being chased. *I* was chasing after whatever had chased me before. I found myself on the other end of the street, running in the opposite direction than I had in previous dreams. It was dusk, and the sky was darkening. I could barely make out what it was that I was running after. It felt enormous in energy and almost frightened me. Might it be too large for me to conquer? I got closer and realized it was a creature or maybe even an animal of some sort. I couldn't get a clear picture because twilight slipped into darkness.

As we came to the bend in the road, the street name changed to the name of the street my grandmother's house stood on, and the creature jumped onto one of the houses. It was massive in size, so easily leaped up and onto the roof. As it reached the top, it turned and made its way down towards me.

I could see it now. Finally make out what it was. As the day fully transitioned into evening, the colors of this creature glowed vibrantly in contrast to the night sky behind it. It was a tiger, a huge tiger running towards me! Its colors of red, orange, and yellow were magnified and shined brightly. It was as if the colors of its fur were alive. Its aura danced vivaciously around him. I was no longer afraid. As it approached me at full speed, I headed towards him at full throttle.

About to clash into one another at that bend, he stopped short and slowly walked up to me and bowed his head. I bowed towards him as well. As he raised his head back up, he slowly moved next to me. As we stood side-by-side, my tiger looked up at me with reverence, and seemed to motion me to continue on. We didn't run; we walked and enjoyed our pace without feeling rushed, hurrying to make a certain schedule. I was no longer afraid. I felt peace and power come over me.

Advancing along the street, we came across my grandmother's house where my family and others from my life were visible through the window. They seemed to be enjoying themselves at what appeared to be a party. I looked and thought, I could show them my tiger and finally receive praise and approval. I turned to my tiger. He was beautiful. As I paused to admire him, I knew I didn't need to go into my grandmother's house anymore. I didn't need them to see how great and beautiful my tiger was. I shrugged my shoulders and sighed deeply. I felt good inside, simply good. I had discovered my tiger and how beautiful and powerful it truly was. That was all I needed. I continued on my journey with my tiger, with power and grace, never looking back.

From then on, in the brilliant light of day, fully awake, with a little bit of grace, I've never looked back. Only forward, steadfastly mastering the Self and consciously taking command of perfection in my life.

Epilogue

"I felt you as soon as you walked in. I know you are true healer. You need to start healing again, and you need to do it now."

She had just finished clearing my energy after reading my cards and relaying a couple urgent messages from Spirit. I had been introduced to Alessandra by my friend Victoria. She relayed the same messages I've received from Spirit since I was a child. However, this time, it felt more direct, and carried a sense of importance and urgency that I needed to start healing again *now*.

I wasn't surprised by what she had to tell me. In the last couple of months I've been contacted by Spirit through a dream and through an actual physical experience in a waking moment, relaying that exact message.

I had dreamt that I was in a huge building near the ocean, and people were in line to receive healing. My mother and my friend, Marie, were there performing the healings. As I started to walk away, I heard a voice asking me not to go. As I turned around, a dazzling ball of light spoke, as it did in dreams past.

"Don't go. You need to go in there and heal."

"I'm focusing on my book at the moment. My mom and Marie, well, they've got this."

"No, your book is already complete. Your healing is part of your purpose as well. And you need to go back in there and heal these people. You need to show your mother and Marie how to heal. It's always been in your hands. You've always known how to bless."

I trusted in those words, therefore, I made my way back inside the house. And as I hovered my hands over a person to heal them, a luminous white light appeared almost blinding me as it filled the entire room. I awoke from that dream aware of the message being given to me by Spirit. But still I avoided the practice out of a lack of confidence.

I went to see a psychic friend of mine, Rose, to help me gain clarity regarding my dream. She confirmed what I intuitively felt about it. I was, indeed, being told to do more healings.

"Now that the book is written and all you need to do is edit, you can go back to the practice and go deeper with the healings. However, they are telling me that you'll be writing your second book even before your first one comes out. In fact, YOU (points up) will be writing it."

"Wait, what do you mean by *me*...that *I* will be writing it? Of course I'll be writing it, but why are you pointing up?"

"Because you won't be writing it, YOU will be writing it..." she said as she widened her eyes, raised both brows while continuing to point up and smirking as if it was a huge inside joke that I didn't get."

How interesting, that's exactly what Mama Jean did. She said that there was one up there, while pointing up, that was like me. Could they be talking about the same thing?

"They tell me that you'll be working with another Master. But they won't let me tell you who exactly that Master is. It's not time yet. But you'll soon find out."

"Wait a minute, you can't tell me that and then not tell me the rest. That's mean and a bit of a torture. Come on! Tell me what the name starts with at least."

Rose paused for a minute as she continued to smile and said, "They won't let me tell you the name, but they will let me tell you what it starts with. It starts with a C..."

Whoa, isn't that exactly what Mama Jean had told me 13 years ago? Same exact details. But how could this be? Rose and Mama Jean don't know one another and over a decade has passed since that first message was given.

"They're telling me that right now, even if you look and research far and wide for Masters whose names start with a C, you'll never find this Master until it is time. It will come to you when the timing is right. You'll know. You won't find it anywhere else outside of you."

"Hmm...okay, fair enough. However, you're telling me I need to go and start healing again, huh? Maybe I'll focus on that after my book is published..."

A few weeks after that first dream, I had been wide awake one night and was finally making my way to bed at 2 o'clock in the morning. Before I slipped into bed, I stood in front of my window and looked out towards the stars. *What am I supposed to be doing now?* I called out to the Ascended Masters and asked for clarity and a sign.

Dear Masters, Mighty I Am Presence, what is it that I'm supposed to be working on at the moment? What's next on this journey besides my book?

I stared at the stars in hopes of receiving a sign from the Masters in the twinkling sky. When I felt the energy shift and knew that my message had been received, I trusted that my question would soon be answered.

I closed the window and the curtains, turned off the lights and hopped into bed. As I lay there, I turned to my husband who had long been asleep and saw he was sweating under the comforter, so I was puzzled why he had it up to his chin. I sat up and started to push the comforter down to my feet. Like magic, my hands lit up with white-silvery light.

At first I thought that maybe my cell phone was underneath the comforter. But then I quickly remembered I had set it on my nightstand to charge. The light filled my hands for awhile and then went away, and then came back, longer each time. It happened three times. It wasn't a light from outside or inside the room. The hue and brightness of the light was different, almost blinding, unlike any other light I had seen in my waking moments.

It was coming from my hands. It was what Spirit and the Ascended Masters had always told me, "It's in your hands; you know how to bless…"

Made in the USA
San Bernardino, CA
16 March 2019